£1-50

949834

GW00993279

The Victorian Day series sets out not only to teach history but to bring it to life by tracing the daily routine of a typical individual.

The 'heroine' of this story is 15-year-old Ellen Hunt, a servant in a large house in Kensington in the 1880s. It is not a typical day. The entire household is busily preparing for a grand dinner party, and Ellen becomes involved in a misunderstanding that threatens her position and her whole future.

Ellen's story is told in a lively, highly readable style. The book's final chapter, 'The National Scene', provides a wealth of authoritative background material, which includes an extremely informative survey of methods of recruiting servants, and a fascinating account of the conditions under which they lived and worked. This section will be invaluable to teachers and students of nineteenth-century social history, and will be a very useful source of ideas for CSE project work. It is followed by suggestions for further reading.

Leonore Davidoff is a lecturer in social history at the University of Essex. Ruth Hawthorn is a former teacher. Both have been engaged in social history research projects.

UNWIN VICTORIAN DAY SERIES : 4

A Day in the Life of a Victorian Domestic Servant

UNWIN VICTORIAN DAY SERIES
Series Editor: Frank E. Huggett

A Day in the Life of
A VICTORIAN
DOMESTIC
SERVANT

LEONORE DAVIDOFF &
RUTH HAWTHORN

LONDON · GEORGE ALLEN & UNWIN LTD
Ruskin House   Museum Street

First published in 1976

© George Allen & Unwin (Publishers) Ltd, 1976

ISBN 0 04 942142 5 hardback
0 04 942143 3 paperback

Filmset in 12 on 13 point Baskerville
Printed in Great Britain
by Cox & Wyman Ltd, London, Fakenham and Reading

Contents

Illustrations

Acknowledgements

Our thanks are due to the following for permission to use illustrations: the Librarian, Barnardo's, Ilford, no. 22; Essex County Records Office, Spalding Collection, no. 18; Faber & Faber, nos 12a and 12b; the Greater London Council (*Survey of London*, vol. 38, *The Museums Area of South Kensington*), nos 1a and 1b; the Master and Fellows of Trinity College, Cambridge, for material from the Munby Collection, nos 3, 4a, 4b, 9a, 9b, 17 and 19; the Museum of London, no. 13; National Monuments Record, no. 7; Radio Times Hulton Picture Library, nos 6 and 8; Science Museum, nos 5, 23a, 23b, 23c and 23d; W. Eglon Shaw, the Sutcliffe Gallery, Whitby, no. 20; Victoria and Albert Museum, no. 11.

Other illustrations are taken from *Mrs Beeton's Household Management* and *The Army and Navy Stores Catalogue* for 1907. The material on the back of the cover is reproduced by kind permission of the Barnet Museum.

Preface

On an evening in October 1860, a scullery maid was washing up in a dirty, evil-smelling cellar:

'She stood at a sink behind a wooden dresser backed with choppers and stained with blood and grease, upon which were piles of coppers and sauce-pans that she had to scour, piles of dirty dishes that she had to wash. Her frock, her cap, her face and arms were more or less wet, soiled, perspiring and her apron was a filthy piece of sacking, wet and tied round her with a cord. The den where she wrought was low, damp, ill-smelling; windowless, lighted by a flaring gas-jet: and, full in view, she had on one side a larder hung with raw meat, on the other a common urinal; besides the many ugly, dirty implements around her.'[1]

This scene was noted down by the Victorian poet A. J. Munby in his diary. He was unusual because very few people of his time took an interest in the conditions in which domestic servants lived and worked.

Yet in the nineteenth century more people were employed in domestic service than in any other occupation except farm work. Millions and millions of women and girls spent long periods living and working as servants. But we know very little about their lives because no one took the trouble to find out anything about them. For the Victorians, a woman's place was in the home, and since servants worked in private homes, doing 'woman's' work, they were not seen as a problem to be discussed in public.

The few people who did write about servants were employers who were worried about the difficulties of finding and managing servants. They had no wish to raise questions about the wider effects of having servants to do their cooking and housework or look after their children. They often tried to hide their uneasiness by writing about servants in an amusing way—servants were thought to be funny. In any case, servants were the responsibility of women and women's concerns were not considered to be very important.

So most of our ideas about life in service come from novels, plays and television. But what was it really like to earn your living in service? This book tells the story of a day in the life of Ellen Hunt, an imaginary but typical domestic servant in a wealthy household in Kensington in the 1880s. Only

[1] A. J. Munby, *Diaries 1860*, vol. 7, Trinity College Collection, p. 79.

a few servants, however, worked in 'gentry' houses with large staffs living apart in their own world of the servants' hall. The majority spent their working lives in households where they were the only servant, sharing the housework with the wife (and older daughters). (See Chapter 8, page 73.)

In the final chapter, 'The National Scene', you will find more information about service in other kinds of households.

1. *THE EARLY HOURS*

Ellen woke up suddenly, out of a deep sleep. Somehow she knew she was late, and that it was especially important not to be late today. She found herself out of bed almost before she was awake, getting dressed in the half-light, with rapid, fumbling movements. She wore cotton combinations next to her skin, and over them she put on her corset. Then came long cotton knickers which buttoned at her waist and a kind of short vest called a spencer. Then came a flannel petticoat, and she had to wear thick black stockings that fastened to the legs of her corset. Her morning uniform was a blue cotton print frock, which came down to her ankles. She took it from its hook, behind a curtain that hung across one corner of her room and served as a wardrobe. She had to be very careful not to wake Rose Simmons, the house parlour-maid, who was asleep in the bed next to hers in their small, sparsely furnished attic bedroom.

She tied a white apron on over her dress, and put a heavy brown apron on over that. Then she had to put up her hair. This was difficult to do quickly. All servants had to wear their hair up, even if they were only twelve or thirteen. Ellen had been taught to do it by a friend in her last job, but she still found it hard. She wound up her long brown hair which reached almost to her waist and curled it into a bun, sticking it with hair pins to keep it in place. She went to the plain wooden wash-stand, which had a white enamel jug and basin standing on it, and poured a little cold water from the jug into the basin. She splashed some of this on her face, then peered into the mirror on the chest of drawers to check that her hair looked reasonably tidy. Then, opening the door as quietly as possible, she went out on to the narrow, dark landing. It was just after six o'clock.

Ellen was fifteen years old. She worked as a between maid, or 'tweeny', in a large house in Kensington. Tweenies were servants who did some of their work for the cook and some of their work under the direction of the parlour-maid; they were shared between the kitchen and the house side. Her employers, Mr and Mrs Parker, kept three other full-time servants, a cook, a house parlourmaid, and a nurse, and had a part-time odd-job man, Mr Pike, who did the especially heavy or dirty work. He had been in the army until he got too old. Now he had to earn a living as best he could. The Parkers had a daughter, Frances, who was just seventeen, two sons who were away at boarding school, a third son Henry who was still at home in the care of Nurse, and another daughter, Elizabeth, who was still only a baby. It was a much smaller establishment than at Ellen's last job, which was in a large country house near her parents' village, and she had only been with the Parkers for six months. Before, she had been employed as a scullery maid, and had spent most of her time just washing up. It was promotion to work as a tweeny. You got more chance to learn the skills needed in the kitchen, and you learned a bit about personal service on the house side as well.

This house had six floors, if you included the attic and the basement. Ellen and Rose, the parlourmaid, slept in a small room in the attic. Nurse's room and the nursery were on the third floor. The master and mistress had their bedroom on the second floor, as did Miss Frances, and the first floor was mainly taken up by the drawing-room. On the ground floor was the dining-room and Mr Parker's study, and in the basement were the kitchen and the scullery. There was another, smaller sitting-room for Mrs Parker at the back of the house between the ground and the first floors, known as the boudoir.

Ellen crept down through the dark, silent building. She stopped outside the main bedrooms to collect the boots or shoes that had been left there. She had to be especially careful and quiet on the upper floors, but when she got to the second floor she went through a door covered with green baize, on to the back stairs, and then she could move faster, without fear of disturbing, or worse, meeting anyone. She ran down the three remaining flights to the basement. Here there was a stone corridor running the length of the house. One of the doors off it led to the kitchen, another to the scullery. Straight ahead of her was the larder, and the door out into the area (as the outside steps were called that came down from street level). Behind her, at the back, was the door leading out to the small garden at the rear of the house. Ellen left the shoes in the dark scullery for the odd-job man to clean, then opened the kitchen door.

In one way, she was glad she wasn't the first down, because if she had been there would have been a scurry of blackbeetles across the tiled floor, and they gave her the horrors. However hard you cleaned the rooms down there, they came back, creeping in from the area. But Ellen should have been first down, and she knew she'd get into trouble for being late.

Sure enough, Cook was there already, impatiently banging at the kitchen range with a menacing metal bar. Ellen braced herself.

'Who do you think *you* are, coming down at ten past six, today of all days. I've enough to do worrying about this evening, without doing all your work as well!'

Cook was generally cross in the mornings. In a household of that size she really should have had a kitchen maid to help her, that is, a girl who could

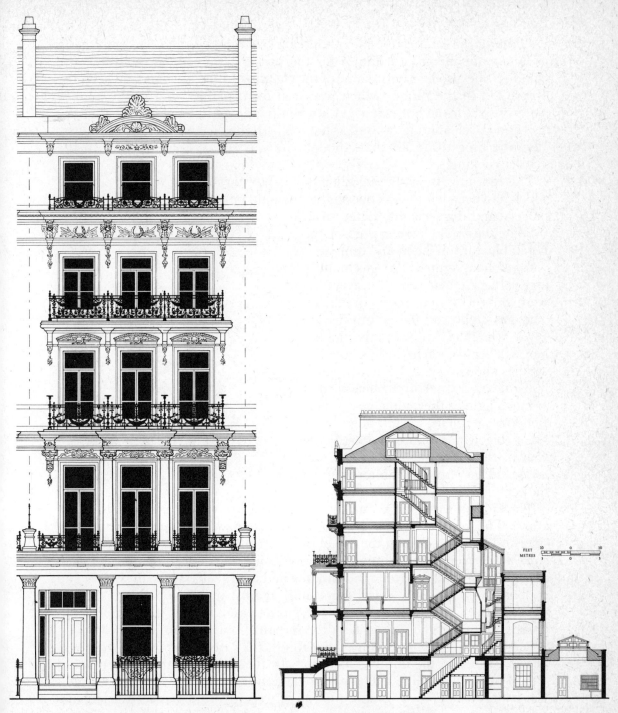

1*a, b* Queen's Gate, London. Architect's drawing of a London house similar to the Parkers' but slightly larger

have helped her all day, instead of just a tweeny who could only work some of the time in the kitchen. Cook was always overworked. She had to prepare breakfast, luncheon and dinner for the nursery, the dining-room and the servants. She also had to do some of the cleaning in the kitchen, and keep the fires alight in the range (which was used for cooking), and in the donkey boiler (used for the hot water). A kitchen maid would have looked after the fires and the cleaning, as well as helped with the cooking. Ellen just did not have the time to do all that, though she was responsible for some of the simpler cooking.

This morning, for example, Ellen hurried to start the big kettle of porridge which had been left to soak overnight. It would be served for breakfast for the nursery and the servants. Later on in the day, she would have to prepare the vegetables for luncheon and dinner.

Cook had lighted the gas mantle above the kitchen table, and was at work on the dining-room breakfast. The gas light seemed a miracle to Ellen who had known only the oil lamps of her last job in Suffolk, and the candles and rush-lights of her parents' house nearby. Cook and Ellen needed as much light as they could get in their London basement, for although there was a big window into the area, the wall of the area was only a few feet away and very little light filtered down to them.

The kitchen was a big room, the same size as the dining-room on the floor above. The range took up nearly the whole of one wall. It had ovens on either side, and hot plates along the top of the central coal fire; the heavy cast iron stove was covered with shiny steel decorations that had to be cleaned each morning. The wall opposite the window had a large dresser with shelves and cupboards for the china and glass built against it, and on the next wall, opposite the range, was a door to the passage and a great many more cupboards. In one of those were kept the servants' sewing things in workboxes. When they weren't busy doing other things they were supposed to get these out and work on the family's mending. In the middle of the kitchen was a huge wooden deal table which had to be scrubbed white every day, for on it Cook did all her work. Beside the range were two old battered armchairs where Cook and Ellen sat in the afternoon and evening when they had a moment off from work.

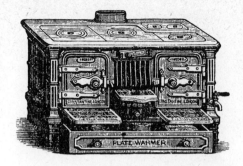

2 Constantine's Treasure Range (no. 84) with roaster and oven, from *Mrs Beeton's Household Management*, 1888

Cook was a short, heavily built woman in her middle age. Ellen thought she had been married, but had never heard her mention her husband, so she assumed that he had died. Cook was strong-minded, and sometimes cross, but she was usually reasonable. She was a good cook, and felt sure of herself, so she didn't often get ruffled. Ellen much preferred working for her than working for Rose, on the house side. Rose was a younger woman, about thirty, and always seemed to be giving orders. Ellen thought she wanted people to notice how efficient she was, and it often made working for her very difficult, as it was to be today.

This was Ellen's third job in service. When she first left her village board school at twelve she worked for a few months as a general daily servant to the village shopkeeper in her parents' own village in Suffolk, a job called by the villagers a 'petty place'. That had been really hard work. She was supposed to clean and help with the cooking, as well as serve in the shop. She had liked the old shopkeeper and his wife, but there was just too much work to do. She had even had to do most of the family's washing. Here at the Parkers' everything was sent out to a local washerwoman. It was Rose's job to get it ready on Monday and check it when it came back on Friday. Ellen only got £2 10s a year at the shopkeeper's, but she looked on it as a sort of apprenticeship, as she wouldn't have got her next job if she hadn't been through that experience. She stayed until there was a vacancy at nearby Bewick Hall for a scullery maid, and she was at the Hall for just over a year. There they kept nearly a full staff of servants including several gardeners and grooms. She earned more there, £7 a year, as well as her board and uniform. But last April, she had heard about this job in London through the vicar's wife, and had decided to come, even though it meant being so far from home. For one thing, she rather hoped some day to become a cook, but most of all she would earn £12 a year with a whole week's holiday.

Tonight, Tuesday, 13th October 1885, there was going to be a dinner party. Ellen had been helping Cook for two days with the preparations, and she was to help Rose serve it this evening. That was really frightening: she had helped at family meals before, and had brought up the food for Rose to serve

17

3   A scullery maid, 1870. Photograph by A. J. Munby

when there were guests (called 'donkeying'), but helping at your first dinner party was like appearing for the first time on stage, out front, with all lights and eyes directed on you. This afternoon, she was to spend some time with

Rose, learning just what she would have to do. And there would be extra work with Cook, helping with the last-minute preparations. It promised to be a full day.

Ellen stirred the porridge until it was just simmering, and then went out to the scullery to prepare for the real work of the day. The scullery was mostly taken up with a large stone sink and draining-board, and the donkey boiler. This was a small temperamental stove above which rested the hot water tank, which they called the copper. The water for the bathroom was heated in it, but there was a tap in the side where you could draw off hot water for other purposes. On either side of the boiler were two large cupboard doors, one of which led to the broom cupboard. The broom cupboard was Ellen's own department. There were buckets, mops, brooms and scrubbing brushes, soap, flannels, rags: everything you needed for cleaning was stored in it. The soap was yellow, in long square bars. If you worked in a good house you cut off what you wanted each day, like a piece of cheese. Ellen knew that she was lucky that way, because in some houses the mistress gave you a small ration of soap each week, insisting that you must keep the house spotless with that! On the shelves were rows of bottles, containing all sorts of mixtures for cleaning different things. Most of them were home made and home bottled, and they were all clearly labelled. As well, there were pots of beeswax, blacking and blacklead, and the boot-cleaning things, metal polish and furniture polish, stored very methodically.

Ellen selected an armful of stiff and soft brushes, dusters and dustpan, and checked that her 'housemaid's box' contained everything that she needed for the grates. She set off again up the back stairs to the dining-room. She had to start here, because Rose would soon be laying out breakfast on the enormous satiny polished table, and the family would want to come down to a room already well warmed. So Ellen first swept the carpet with a stiff  brush, brushing all the crumbs over towards the fireplace. Then she laid a large piece of pale heavy canvas over the part of the carpet nearest the grate, and put her box down on it. She swept out the grate and put all the ashes from yesterday's fire in the bucket that Mr Pike had already put there for her this morning. She kept the embers from the old fire separate, as these would go on the kitchen fire.

Then she brushed the grate, rubbed blacking on the black parts and polished them. The shiny parts she just rubbed with a duster today, though some days she went over them with emery powder, a sort of fine grey sand that brought up a polish on steel. Then she laid the new fire and lit it. This was quite a skill in itself, but Ellen had learnt to do it at a very early age from her mother, and thought nothing of it. She was just thankful that Mr Pike got up

4a Seven in the morning
Photographs by A. J. Munby, 1872

4b Seven in the evening

20

so early and was able to get the coal box filled by the time she came to do the fires.

While the fire was getting under way, Ellen took a clean duster and rubbed the wooden parts of the furniture. The table was a huge area which had to have a perfectly even polish all over it, and there was nothing for it but just hard rubbing on the french polished surface. It was always covered by two, and sometimes three, cloths at mealtimes, but it still had to be perfect underneath.

By this time the fire was burning brightly, and Ellen gathered up the ash bucket, her canvas and her housemaid's box, and scuttled up the front stairs to her mistress's boudoir. This was a smaller and more friendly room than the grand drawing-room on the first floor, and for that reason tended to be where the family gathered on normal days to sit, though it was meant to be a retreat for Mrs Parker in the way that the study was for her husband. Ellen went through the same jobs here as she had in the dining-room.

When she had finished, she looked round to make absolutely sure she had not left anything lying around. She could just imagine the mistress finding a duster on the floor, and the idea made her shudder.

The last cleaning job before breakfast was the front steps. She hated this because it meant going out in full view of the whole street. Ellen put her housemaid's box back in the broom cupboard, and took out a bucket. This she filled with warm water from the copper, and carried it up the kitchen stairs again, together with brushes and other equipment needed for the steps and the front door. She brushed down the door first, and polished the big brass knocker and the letter-box. Next the steps had to be washed, and then rubbed with hearthstone powder to make them white. There were five ordinary stone steps and at the bottom there was a long one that curled round the rest at either side. It was a simple enough job in itself, but the problem was that to do it you had to kneel, bending over, and stay in this undignified position for the passers-by to see. It was the delight of all the errand boys in London to think up jokes to make about the maids doing the front steps. But it wasn't the errand boys she minded so much. In fact, if you were in service you would quite likely marry an errand boy because you didn't have a chance to meet many others. What really worried her was the idea that a gentleman might look, and perhaps say something. She had been told about gentlemen taking advantage of girls, perhaps offering them money, and she was afraid she wouldn't know what to say. But even the errand boys were a nuisance. Ellen wasn't old enough to think of flirting with them, and her main object was to get through the steps as quickly as possible.

Most jobs in service had very strict rules against 'followers'. Even if Ellen had made friends with one of the boys she met, she would have had to keep the friendship secret, otherwise she could have lost her place. Of course many girls did have followers, and often their employers knew of it and overlooked it. But it was still officially forbidden; sometimes other servants would tell on girls they had a grudge against. You had to be very careful.

Down in the kitchen Ellen found Cook had been getting the tea trays ready. There was one each for the master and Miss Frances, with the best china and a plate of thinly sliced bread and butter. There was also one for Nurse, with ordinary china. Rose would be down any minute now, and her first job of the day was to take these trays up. Ellen went out to the scullery to collect the boots. Sure enough, Mr Pike had cleaned them and left them in a neat row next to the boiler. Ellen didn't have to take Nurse's or the children's, but she collected up the master's and mistress's shoes, and Miss Frances's, and took them upstairs. She left them outside the doors where she had collected them earlier. Then she had to come down again for the hot water cans. They had to be taken upstairs for the women of the house to wash with. They were rather like stumpy watering cans, with spouts, and Ellen could not manage more than two at a time when they were full. She took two out to the scullery and filled them from the copper, gave a quick stir to the porridge which was almost burning, and set off again up the back stairs for the nursery.

It was almost exactly half past seven.

2. BREAKFAST

There was still no sign of life from the second floor, but on the stairs to the third floor Ellen met Rose coming down. They were outside Miss Frances's room, so they couldn't make any noise, but Rose gave her a critical looking-over: she was responsible for Ellen's appearance in the 'front' rooms, the ones where the family went, and she took this duty, like her others, seriously. Ellen must have looked all right this morning, for Rose gave her a tight-lipped nod and passed on downstairs to get the tea trays.

Ellen arrived at the nursery door and put one can down. With her free hand she tapped quietly, then opened the door, picked up the other half of her load and went in. It was a light room, and warm even at this hour of the day in October because Nurse had to see to it that the fire stayed in all night. It was her job to look after the younger children of the family, and do the daily cleaning in the nursery. In a larger household she would have had a nursery maid to help her with the children and to do all the cleaning. Here she had to make do with Mr Pike's help in bringing up coal for the fires, and Ellen's help in the fortnightly thorough clean, or 'doing out' of the nursery rooms. Nurse herself had started as a nursery maid, and had learnt her job that way: when she had felt sure enough of herself she had applied for a full nurse's job.

She had looked after all the Parker children in their turn, but at the moment she had only Henry, aged seven, and baby Elizabeth, aged eighteen months. She would be losing Henry next year when he went away to school like his two brothers, and then her life would become easier. Her main problem was what she would do when Elizabeth grew up. People liked to keep the same nurse for all their children, just as the Parkers had done. But Nurse would be in her fifties then, and she knew that a young couple would hesitate before taking on someone so old. Some families found a way of keeping on their nurse when the children had grown up, but the Parkers wouldn't be able to afford it. She hoped that Miss Frances might take her on for her own children when she married. But what if she didn't? If she couldn't get another job as a nurse, her prospects were poor; she would have to end her working life in some much harder job, perhaps as a washerwoman, and when she grew too infirm to do that there was always the threat of the workhouse. That seemed a long way from this pleasant warm nursery in Kensington, but Nurse knew what a real possibility it was.

Nurse had put a zinc bath tub in front of the fire for the hot water that Ellen would bring. The bath tub was surrounded with clothes horses draped with towels, put out to protect Elizabeth from draughts, as well as to warm the towels to dry her with afterwards. On the far side of the room, in front of the window, Ellen could see the old family rocking horse. Elizabeth was stumping about with an ivory teething ring in one hand, trying to push the clothes horses over. She was so hampered by all the layers of clothes she had on that there wasn't any danger of her getting very far. She was protected from the fire by a tall fender with a padded seat running round the top. Henry was sitting on this, still in his night shirt, trying to catch hold of Elizabeth as she went past without having to go to the trouble of moving himself. He stuck his tongue out at Ellen when he saw her.

Nurse took the cans and said 'Thank you, dear,' in a kindly way. Ellen left quickly, shutting the door behind her. She went all the way down to the basement again, filled another can of water and collected her housemaid's box, and made another trip upstairs. She went up to Miss Frances's room, put down the box, knocked, and without waiting for an answer, went in, leaving the box on the landing. The tea tray was standing untouched on the table by Miss Frances's bed. Ellen put the can down by the wash-stand. There was a stirring movement from under the heap of bedclothes on the bed, and Ellen gently called 'It's twenty to eight, Miss Frances' before gathering up the empty hot water can from last night and making for the door. There was a muffled grunt.

Miss Frances had had her seventeenth birthday the week before and the dinner party this evening was really in her honour. She was definitely becoming a young lady now: next April she would be presented at Court. Since Ellen had been in this job, Miss Frances had changed a good deal, from a schoolgirl into a young woman. She had begun to coil up her long hair into a bun; her skirts had been lengthened from just below the knee to the floor and she was allowed to dine with her parents in the evening. Today was a landmark that meant almost as much to Ellen as it did to Miss Frances, for although the dinner nearly doubled her usual workload, Ellen was very excited about it. It had been something different to look forward to.

She took up her box again and went down to light the fire in the master's dressing-room. She didn't need to bring hot water for him, for he had recently taken to using the new bathroom, and Ellen welcomed the change. In fact, he and the servants were the only ones who did use it. Every week, Rose would let the others know when they could go and have a bath without there being any chance of meeting one of the family. The ladies of the family always washed in their rooms, as it was more modest.

Mrs Parker had her breakfast in bed, and wouldn't need her water until after she got up, so for now there was just the master's fire to do. As Ellen was finishing the fire, Rose came in to lay out the master's clothes for the day and straighten the brushes which were arranged on top of the chest of drawers. She also ran a duster round the ornaments on the mantelpiece.

'Mind you don't leave those cans behind,' said Rose, and her voice had a nagging edge to it. Like Cook, Rose's main problem was that she was always under pressure, and she gave vent to this by going on at Ellen, just as the parlourmaid had always gone on at *her* when she was a tweeny.

Households varied, of course, but there was always a tendency to employ as few servants as possible, and sometimes fewer. Both Mr Parker and the mistress had grown up in very wealthy homes where there had been more than enough money for a full staff, so they both had very high standards about the amount of work that should be done. Unfortunately Mr Parker was not the oldest son, and now he had to earn his own living. This meant that he could not afford a large full-time staff; and worse for those he did employ, he would not pay for extra labour when there were special occasions, like today. So then everyone had extra work, on top of their full timetables. A wealthier employer would have got in a kitchen maid for the day, as well as experienced staff to wait at table in the evening. Instead, Cook and Rose had to carry the extra responsibility. Ellen knew that even though Rose was always telling her to do things, it wasn't because Rose was lazy herself. So she hurried up and left with all her belongings, just as Rose was knocking on the master's and mistress's bedroom door. 'Just before eight o'clock, sir,' she called, clearly and firmly.

Back in the scullery, Ellen's next job was to take up the nursery breakfast tray. She put her housemaid's box away in the cupboard, washed her hands in the sink and took off the dirty top apron, before fetching a large tray and putting it on the kitchen table ready for loading. This was for Nurse's tea and the children's milk, as well as porridge and a dish of kedgeree, plates and cups. Cook was busy at the range where she had several saucepans simmering, and as Ellen left with her burden Cook had started to make the tea for the dining-room. By the time Ellen had delivered the nursery food and returned with the empty water cans Cook had arranged several covered silver dishes on another tray. Rose was there, checking it over before she carried it up to the

5   The kitchen. A drawing from *Modern Domestic Cookery* by Mrs Rundell, 1855

dining-room. Mr Parker and Miss Frances would have the choice of kedgeree, grilled kidneys and boiled eggs for their breakfast. Rose would serve it at half past eight.

At least here there were no family prayers to interrupt the morning's work as there had been at Bewick Hall. There, after nursery breakfast had been served, at 8.30 promptly, Albert, the footman, rang the big gong in the hall, and the whole household, master, mistress, children, servants and guests if there were any, filed into the dining-room where the chairs were set in rows. Ellen sat right at the back with the youngest servants; the family sat towards the front. At the head of the table the master read a passage from the Bible, then they all turned and knelt before their chairs to pray. At first Ellen had felt very strange being in the room with the master and mistress. The house-keeper had always checked to see if the maids' uniforms were clean, their caps straight. At the Parkers' there were family prayers only on Sunday evenings. Often the Parkers were out anyway and Ellen was rather thankful, for Mrs Parker was strict about asking her Bible texts.

When Rose had left for the dining-room to arrange the dishes on a stand warmed by a spirit light, Ellen and Cook sat down to their breakfast at the kitchen table. They drank cocoa at breakfast. Cook poured it out while Ellen served them both with a helping of her porridge. It wasn't too bad, after all. They had sugar and some creamy milk, and Ellen couldn't find any lumps in hers. Cook took the opportunity to remind Ellen of her duties for the day.

'That Rose said she wouldn't need you so long for cleaning this morning so you could come down earlier and start on tonight's vegetables. But make sure you aren't around in your mucky apron when the mistress comes down. We'll be all right so long as she doesn't go changing anything at the last minute but it's only thanks to me planning it all in advance.' Cook sniffed with satisfaction and finished her porridge. 'Have a look in the kedgeree saucepan. I didn't send it all up. There'll be enough for us to have a taste and still leave some for her.' 'Her' was Mrs Parker.

Cook always managed to see that they ate well in the kitchen. When Ellen had first gone to work at Bewick Hall she had been amazed by the large size of the helpings at meals, compared with what they could afford at home. And since she had come here she had tasted food she had never heard of before. At the Hall the servants had completely separate food from that eaten in the dining-room, but here Cook saw to it that they had something similar to that which was served to the Parkers.

They finished eating quickly, each of them thinking about the next job. Cook would start work cleaning the kitchen, and Ellen would see to the washing up. She had to fetch down the nursery tray, and help Rose clear the dining-room table. She took the dirty things out to the scullery and got through that job rapidly, to be ready when Rose came to fetch her for the next one.

She and Rose had to go up together with the mistress's breakfast tray. Rose carried the tray, prepared by Cook with silver dishes and the fine breakfast china, and Ellen carried her housemaid's box and the slop pail. When they reached the mistress's room, Ellen knocked and opened the door, holding it for Rose to go in first. While Rose put down the tray and drew back the heavy brocade curtains, Ellen shut the door and got to work on the fireplace. She swept it out quickly, and laid and lit a new fire, as Rose helped the mistress sit up in bed, arrange her nightcap and smooth the covers. Rose put the tray across the mistress's knees. Ellen worked so fast that the two servants were ready to leave the room together. Rose went downstairs to get her brushes and dusters to do the lighter work of cleaning the ornaments and tabletops in the dining-room and drawing-room. Ellen went upstairs, to clean out Miss Frances's room. Later, Rose would go back to help the mistress dress.

Ellen knocked here too, just in case Miss Frances had come back upstairs for some reason after breakfast; but there was no answer, so she went in with her box and got to work. She stripped the bed, turned the mattress and then remade the bed. She emptied the soapy water from the basin on the wash-stand into the slop bucket, and, gritting her teeth, stooped down and reached under the bed for the chamber pot. There was a lavatory on the same floor, but there was no question of Miss Frances going along to use it at night. It was the tweeny's job to clean away the slops so neither the other servants nor their employers gave any more thought to the question. Ellen rinsed out the chamber pot, using water from the jug on the wash-stand; then she gave it a wipe with a cloth dampened with vinegar which she kept in a bottle in her housemaid's box. Later she would empty the slop pail down the lavatory. When she had dusted the room, tidied away Miss Frances's

night-dress and straightened her dressing-table, she went up to the attic bedrooms and got to work on them. This was quicker, as there was much less furniture and few knick-knacks (Mrs Parker didn't approve of them for servants), and she could move around faster.

Ellen was about half way through brushing down the stair carpet, feeling very hot and sticky from the work, when Rose called to her from the landing below.

'Ellen!' she hissed in a fierce stage whisper, 'the mistress would like to see you. Quickly, give me your overall.' Ellen could tell there was something seriously wrong from the fact that she was summoned at all. She was trembling as she knocked at the door of the mistress's bedroom and waited to be called inside.

The mistress was up and dressed, standing with her back to the room and looking at something on her dressing-table. She was a small woman, and quite stout, but she had a dignified way of holding herself. Her dress was of dark brown silk and velvet, cleverly designed so as not to emphasise her unfashionably large waist. Her hair was beginning to go grey and on it she wore a little frilly white cap, pinned at the top of her head.

Ellen shut the door and waited with her hands clasped in front of her. After a few minutes Mrs Parker turned round with a great rustle of petticoats, a gesture which she had perfected over the years to impress both servants and guests. It wasn't wasted on Ellen, who was by now far too frightened to speak: luckily she didn't have to.

'Ellen, I have been looking for a pendant, which I know for a fact was on my dressing-table yesterday morning. Simmons tells me that she knows nothing of it, and as you are the only other person who would have reason to come in here I have naturally called for you to tell me where you have put it. It would be understandable for you to think of putting it away, for it is quite valuable; though I consider it rather beyond your duties. I intend to make a present of it to Miss Frances to wear at dinner this evening, so you see it is important that I have it as soon as possible.'

6 Mistress and servant, 1866

Ellen froze inside. She could see the situation immediately and realised there was nothing she could do. She knew nothing about the pendant and the mistress thought she had stolen it. Cleaning the dressing-table was Rose's responsibility, and it would never occur to Ellen to examine the things laid out on it. She glanced at it now, and saw only a confusion of small framed miniatures and misty photographs, ornaments and bottles, brushes and hand mirrors. The mistress was waiting for an answer, and Ellen began to stammer.

'I never saw it, mum, please. I only do the bed and the fires. I don't know where it is.' In her confusion she was wringing her hands. She knew she should try to be calm and convincing but that only made her more nervous.

'I see,' said the mistress. 'I am disappointed in you, Ellen. We have spent some time already on your moral education at our Sunday prayers, and I think this is a poor way of repaying it. I hope you will think better of it. You can go now. I must think of the best way of dealing with this.'

Ellen left the room in despair. In those few minutes her world had fallen about her ears. She knew that she had not seen the pendant, but it didn't matter who believed her so long as the mistress didn't; for she would lose her position here, and would never get another one. Every employer asked for a reference, or a 'character', from your last employer, and no matter how you explained any misunderstandings you might have had with them, it was the reference that mattered. The only other way to get a job in service was through the agencies, or 'registry offices'. But they only arranged for you to meet a new employer, and she would want a character from your last employer in just the same way. There was no way out. No one would take on a girl with a character like Ellen's would be now.

Ellen finished the stairs, feeling that everything was ruined. She wasn't exactly surprised at the way the mistress had behaved, because she knew from many stories that it was the way that they saw things. With a few exceptions, they didn't really trust servants, or rather, felt they always had to be on the lookout for dishonesty. But it was very important for Ellen to set the record straight, and she thought and thought about it while she was finishing her housework.

On normal days she would have to do the study next. That involved the same work as the other rooms, but in addition had the books. There were bookshelves covering all the walls in the study. Ellen had to take one shelf each day and 'clap' each book to get the dust out of it. But Rose had told her to leave the study today, because of all the extra work.

So the last bit of cleaning was the drawing-room. This room had been 'done out' the day before, so there was not much dust on the carpet or the furniture, but she still went over it carefully. Yesterday Rose had helped her

7   The morning-room of a London house, 1896

HOUSE PARLOUR MAIDS WORK[a]

Well trained servants do not come down in the morning without having washed.

Down 6.30: Sunday 7.30: Pull up Drawing room blinds, open windows. Do fire places if used. Do the Dining room fire place by which time the kettle will be boiling to make the early tea, take up tea 7.O'clock, then sweep up the pieces in Dining room & dust. Lay the cloth for breakfast 8 O'clock, take it in & then go up stairs & strip the beds down, open bed room windows. Have own breakfast. At 9 o'clock clear away breakfast, wash up the breakfast things & put on clean apron, then make the beds. Clean the nickle taps with chamois leather only, wash the baths out & the floors & lavatory basins; then dust every bed room. Little Prentice doing the floors & passage. 12: O'clock do the Cruets, fresh every day.

L2.15: go up & dress, then lay the cloth for Lunch. Wait at table, clear away wash up all glass & silver, put every thing away in its place.

Pantry taps are to be cleaned every day, sink well washed out & floor washed.

Monday
Help Mistress with the Laundry; wash the brushes & combs & turn out Pantry.

Tuesday
Dining room thoroughly turned out. Windows cleaned. Fire place done thoroughly before breakfast.

Wednesday
A bed room & bath room & dressing room one week; spare rooms another & so on.

Thursday
Silver, every bit clean if not finished in the morning the rest in the afternoon.

Friday
W: C: Passage & stairs & Hall.

Saturday
Servants' bed room.

---

[a] By permission of the Barnet Museum.

COOKª

No well trained servant comes down without washing herself

Down 6.30 Sunday 7.30: Open kitchen windows put on kettle for early tea on gas ring, but, this must <u>never</u> be used for anything else, if so it will be cut off. Light kitchen fire & put the milk on in milk boiler & kettle for breakfast. Do the morning room fire & sweep, then put on clean apron & prepare the breakfast, making both the Tea & Coffee & Toast & put ready for Prentice to take in. Get the kitchen breakfast which should be quite finished by 9.o'clock clear it away into the scullery & wash up, then clean the knives & dust put into box ready for Lunch; sweep the kitchen; clean the hearth & scrub the table & be ready for Mistress at quarter to 10: On no account are these rules to be altered, any departure from then will be considered a serious offence & will be dealt with accordingly. Get the lunch ready. Always cook slowly — anything cooked fast is never good, except Boiled Suet Puddings & they should be well covered in water. Spinach cooked in <u>enamel</u> or <u>copper</u> saucepans, never iron. Answer all bells till 1 o'clock & keep the down stairs fires in till 1: O'clock.

Dinner 7: O'clock; Bed at 10. p: m:

Hot bath every Saturday night; outings every Sunday from 3.30 till 10:O'clock, but <u>not</u> an evening a week. A day a month if wanted & summer holiday.

<u>Monday</u>
Table & Dresser drawers cupboards to be thoroughly turned out & relaid with paper. Broom cupboard, Bread box, salt box to be well scrubbed.

<u>Tuesday</u>
The Larder thoroughly turned out & cellar.

<u>Wednesday</u>
Kitchen Dresser.

<u>Thursday</u>
Morning at 6 o'clock clean the flues.

<u>Friday</u>
Clean the kitchen stove before breakfast.

<u>Saturday</u>
Kitchen windows floor & scullery.
The outside to be kept very clean & tidy.

move the furniture to the middle of the room and scatter moist tea leaves all over the carpet. Then Ellen had swept them up, together with the dust they had collected, and the two of them had moved all the furniture back again and really gone over it for marks of all kinds. Rose had dusted the remote corners of the picture frames and the mouldings round the windows. Ellen had also polished the wooden parts of the furniture, while Rose had dusted every single ornament and photograph frame, which were crowded on to all the tables and shelves in the room. This sort of treatment was given to each room every fortnight, and this time it had been arranged to coincide with the dinner party. So today it was only a matter of doing the grate and fire, dusting everything else lightly, and sweeping the carpet. Mr Pike had done this coal box too, so the work didn't take too long. Ellen was thinking all the time about the pendant. Where could it have got to?

When Ellen got downstairs again, Cook was standing in a spotless kitchen, with her hands on her hips, shaking her head. She was upset by the mistress too, but for different reasons.

'She comes down here in the middle of the day, almost, and never at the same time, and expects to find the kitchen like a bloomin' hospital. "I like to see a clean kitchen at least once a day," says she. What does she think I am? It leaves me about five minutes to get the luncheon on. The meals today have all been planned for over a week, so there's no need for her to come down at all. Now, let's get down to it.'

What happened usually was that Cook would sketch out the day's menus and the mistress would come down after breakfast to check them over, and discuss any difficulties in the housekeeping that came up. Some mistresses would check the larder and pantry to see what was left over and plan the meals themselves, but Mrs Parker left all this to Cook. Cook was supposed to have the kitchen spotless by then, and not start work till after the visit. But Mrs Parker was a late riser, and never very punctual once up, so Cook was often kept waiting around during the precious hours of the morning. The first thing she did now was to take Ellen into the larder with her, to get out the things they would need for lunch.

The back of the larder was the coolest place in the house. In fact it was under the road. Even though it was broad daylight outside, they had to light a candle to take in with them, as there was no window. On the back of the larder door there were pinned some yellowing pieces of paper. They were lists of duties of the cook, the tweeny and the parlourmaid written out years ago for earlier cooks and tweenies. Ellen had read them through when she first came, and had been dismayed by the amount of work she was supposed to do. But they were misleading. For example the tweeny should have 'set up' the table for Cook before each meal. This meant putting out all the bowls, spoons, etc. for cooking. It really needed a full-time kitchen maid to do that. The mistress had written the lists out soon after she had got married, and the various servants who had done the jobs had found it easier to share them out in rather different ways. There was another cupboard off the far end of the larder where the master stored his wine. Next to the wine cellar door there was a long slate table, and on it stood the milk jugs and the meat safe. This was a sort of cage made of small mesh wire netting, which allowed air to circulate round the meat but kept the flies off. There was an icebox, for which Cook could have ice delivered, but it was used mostly in the summer for butter, and for special things like ice cream. Milk had to be delivered twice, and sometimes three times a day, because it was so difficult to store it at home. The dairy boy called once in the early morning, with the milk or cream for breakfast. Then he came again in the middle of the morning, and if Cook needed any extra for cooking later in the day she would ask him to come back again in the afternoon. They were going to need it today for all the sauces Cook would make later on for the dinner party.

Ellen loved the smell of the larder, which was a mixture of fresh vegetables and the spiciness of a grocer's shop. Cook kept it beautifully, cleaning it out every day, and nothing stayed in it long enough to get stale. But, just in case, she arranged little pieces of charcoal along the shelves to keep the air especially fresh. She had baked yesterday and there was an earthenware crock full of fresh loaves which added to the sweetness of the air. Ellen held out a tray, and Cook began piling it with all the things that they would need.

3. *LUNCHEON*

'It's no good getting angry about it,' Cook was saying as she stood at the range stirring a large pan. Ellen sat at the kitchen table, trimming broccoli for tonight's dinner and dropping each head into a bowl of water as it was finished. 'They'll always suspect us whatever the truth, and if there's nothing to suspect us of, they'll invent something. Why I was at one place where the missus left a half sovereign under the carpet on purpose. If the housemaid left it then she could accuse her of not sweeping properly and of course if it wasn't returned then the girl'd lose her job.'

Ellen finished the broccoli and started on the large pile of potatoes. When they were peeled she put them in a bucket of water beside her on the floor. She was doing enough for luncheon and dinner at the same time.

'I don't see she had any call to think I'd do such a thing,' she said sadly. 'It stands to reason I'd lose my place and my character, same as Rose would, and they didn't suspect her.'

Ellen didn't know what her mother would say if she went home in disgrace. There wasn't anything else a girl could do at home in the village, and anyway there had been two more little brothers born since Ellen had first gone into service and there wasn't enough room for her in the house. The only other place near home she could get work was the nearby town of Hadleigh. They wouldn't ask for a reference at the mill or for a first position in a shop. But the mill girls weren't really respectable, and there weren't many places in shops; anyway Ellen didn't think she'd be quick enough at her figures to do that. And it would mean travelling from home every day, on foot, probably. Her mother would be sad to see her back, and her father would be angry. He'd always wanted his girls in service.

'I got given notice once,' said Cook. Her thoughts must have been following the same pattern as Ellen's. 'It doesn't have to be the end of the world, like everyone says. I was a kitchen maid then, and I'd hoped to be a cook in my next place. But when I got notice with no character I couldn't hope to do that, of course. What I did was go to the place I'd had before that, and saw the missus there. Luckily for me she was a good sort, and she said she'd give me a character, so when I went for another kitchen maid job I just forgot about the old cat that gave me notice. It was a bad place anyway, that one. I was trying to learn to cook, and the cook that was there was as bad as her missus.

She never let me watch her working, though it was agreed I should be allowed to. She used to think up foolish jobs to get me out of the room just as she was putting the dish together, I had to work twice as hard to try to outwit her. I learnt, though, in spite of her. She didn't want me to get as good as her, and maybe do her out of a job. No fear of that anyway, she'd worked her way in with the missus, and I think it was her doing that got me dismissed.'

'I could never go to the missus at my last place,' said Ellen thinking of the remote and stately lady of Bewick Hall. 'I only saw her to speak to twice all the time I was there; I was only a scullery maid and she didn't know anything about me.'

If you wanted to be a cook, as Ellen did, you would expect to start as a scullery maid, then an assistant kitchen maid, then a kitchen maid and then a cook. She was learning part of a kitchen-maid's job in this place as a tweeny: if all had gone well she could hope to be a kitchen maid next time. Her mother had been a cook. She said it taught you how to manage when you got married. The actual cooking wasn't much help because Ellen's father didn't like the fancy foreign dishes that her mother had learnt to make while she was in service, and anyway they could never afford to buy the things to make them. But her mother was very thorough in her housekeeping and never wasted anything. Ellen could see that it saved the family a lot of money. Mother always said that housemaids only learnt expensive, wasteful ways. And another reason why Ellen preferred the kitchen was that you had less daily contact with 'them'. You could go up the other way, starting as a house-maid and working up to a housekeeper, if you could find the right establish-ment. But that meant closer and closer contact with the people who frightened her most. Anyway, she enjoyed cooking and liked the idea of being like Cook better than that of being like Rose. But what would happen to all those plans now?

Cook had two large chickens boiling for lunch and had put a pudding to steam. Now she was ready for the vegetables, and while she was checking them Ellen took out the saucepans that were already dirty and washed them. The copper ones had to be cleaned with a gritty, slimy mixture of soap and sand; this was hard on the hands and it made the washing-up water unusable for anything else. She used soda for the other pots, and this was bad for the skin too. By the end of the day her hands were often so sore and red it was painful to move her fingers. She had got into the way of spending some of her quarter's wages on a small pot of glycerine to put on her hands at night.

When there were no more dirty pots she went back to the kitchen for her next instructions. There was still half an hour before luncheon would be served in the dining-room. The master had his meal in the city, so there was only the mistress and Miss Frances in the dining-room, Nurse and the children upstairs and the three servants downstairs.

8   Kitchen staff at a big house near Keswick, 1860

Cook set her busy on a job for the evening meal. She showed Ellen how to take each potato and carve it into a perfect small oval. This meant paring away more potato than was actually saved, which seemed to her very wasteful, but Cook told her to put the parings into the pig bucket.

When Ellen had finished that and cleared it away, it was time to get the nursery tray ready. Cook gave Ellen some chicken to mince for the baby, while she put the dishes with their covers on the enormous tray. Ellen added Elizabeth's dish and the plates and cutlery. The cutlery used in the nursery was the same as that used in the kitchen. It was kept in a different cupboard from the silver that was used in the dining-room, and it was made of some dull, plain metal. But it was easier to keep clean. All the knives had to be cleaned and polished once a day by Mr Pike, because the blades would have rusted and stained otherwise. In other houses, very young boys or girls were sometimes hired specially to do this.

Ellen set off upstairs with the tray. While she was putting it down on the nursery table, and Nurse was unloading it, Henry came up to her. He had been having some lessons with his mother that morning, a pastime which she found more trying even than he did, and he was full of the latest gossip.

'Mama says it is wicked to steal, and Mr Allen, the vicar, says that wicked people can't go to heaven when they die: Mama says the tweeny must have taken her necklace, the one she was going to give to Frances. She says you can't get honest servants nowadays.'

Ellen blushed and, not knowing what to say, ran from the room. She could hear Nurse scolding Henry as she hurried downstairs, stopping on the way to see to the dining-room fire. In the kitchen she found Rose and Cook getting the tray ready for the dining-room. Rose didn't have to wait at lunch time; she arranged the dishes, as at breakfast, saw that the mistress and Frances had their first platefuls and then left them to help themselves to the other dishes, as they wanted. Cook had provided them with a chicken, a salad, potatoes, a steamed pudding, jelly and a bowl of fruit. When Rose had done all she needed for the mistress and Miss Frances she came back to join Cook and Ellen, who were setting to work on their own meal. It consisted of the other half of the chicken that had gone up to the nursery, otherwise it was the same food as in the dining-room, without the jelly and fruit. This was their big meal of the day, as it was for the nursery. In the evening they usually had a bread and cheese supper.

They didn't talk much at the meal. This was the time when Ellen missed her old job most. There the servants had a separate dining-room of their own, known as the servants' hall, and there were so many of them sitting down to each meal that it was always very lively. As scullery maid she had had to wait on the other servants, but it was fairly informal and she had been able to sit down with them after she had passed the plates around.

At the Parkers' the servants didn't talk very much. Cook thought that Rose was too 'in' with Mrs Parker and treated her rather like an enemy spy. Rose suspected that Cook and Ellen had jokes about her when she wasn't there. So neither Cook nor Rose ever relaxed in each other's company, and anyway today they both had too much else to occupy their minds. Cook and Rose were drinking beer with their meal; Ellen could have done so, but she preferred water. They were given a little extra money each year as a 'beer allowance' and they used to pool it to buy beer. Ellen felt she ought to put her money in with the others, though she could have used it better by sending it to her family at home.

She hurried her pudding and went off upstairs again to see to the fires before she would have to start on the washing up.

By the time Ellen had got back to the kitchen, Rose had been upstairs to check that Mrs Parker and Miss Frances had finished and left the dining-room. She came down again to report to Ellen that the dining-room was free for Ellen to come and clear the table. Ellen took a large tray up the kitchen stairs, and crossing the hall as quickly as possible, slipped into the dining-room.

She collected up the dirty plates and silver on to her tray, and took them downstairs to the scullery. She filled the sink with hot soapy water, and then a large enamel basin and a small jug. At the bottom of the basin she put a folded teatowel; the silver would be done in the basin, and it mustn't be scratched. The jug was for the knives. She stood them up in it so that the blades were under water but the handles wouldn't get wet, as the water would loosen the glue that held them on.

She had to go up to the top of the house again to get the nursery tray. Luckily Henry was out of the way, supposedly lying down after the meal, and Elizabeth too was having a rest. Nurse must have been in her own room, as the nursery was empty. Ellen collected the dirty things there too, and took them down to the scullery. Then she cleared the dishes from the kitchen table.

She scraped all the leavings off the plates and dishes. Anything remotely edible went into the pig bin, the contents of which were sold to a man who came round every two or three days. Cook was allowed to keep the money from the pig bin; it was known as one of her perquisites, or 'perks' as she called it. Another of her perks was the dripping that came from the roasts, as well as the bones from the meat. These could be sold to men who called round regularly. Not all employers allowed cooks to have these perks, but it was usually expected. Ellen was lucky with this cook because she shared the pig bin money with her, and this was unusual. The other rubbish Ellen put aside to take out to the dust box.

Ellen had learnt to wash up the hard way when she had been a scullery maid. No pans were ever allowed to be left soaking which meant that every-

9a   Hannah, wife of A. J. Munby, dressed
for dirty chores

9b   Hannah as she appeared when serving

thing had to be scoured away. Another difficulty was that sinks in both houses were large shallow stone ones, with rough pitted surfaces that were themselves very hard to keep clean. The water got cold very quickly, and the whole thing became a greasy, gritty mess, with the sand from the copper saucepan mixture. It helped if you moved fast and did things in an exact order. By now Ellen was quite an expert, and got through the dirty work quickly before turning her attention to the silver plate. This required more careful treatment. Each article of plate, like a spoon, or a dish cover, was wiped with a cloth in the water, then dried, and then given a quick rub with a cloth impregnated with a special home-made polish. When she was first shown this system Ellen was dismayed by the work it involved, but she soon realised that in fact it was quicker in the long run than letting the silver gradually lose its sheen and then having to have regular polishing sessions. Albert, the footman at Bewick Hall, had shown her this trick. The plate was carefully wrapped in a green baize cloth afterwards, and put away in a special cupboard in the kitchen which Rose locked up after each meal.

Ellen wiped down the draining-boards, and gave the sink itself and the scullery floor a quick scrub, before making a trip out to the dust box in the yard at the back. The yard was on the same level as the scullery, about fifteen feet wide, and steps led from it up to the small garden at the back of the house. Under these steps was the dust box, a large fixed wooden container like a coal bunker into which they emptied all the rubbish. Mr Pike emptied it when it got full. The last time was the day before yesterday so it was beginning to fill up again. Ellen was just tossing her bundle in when a scrap of brightly coloured tissue paper caught her eye. It looked quite clean. Ellen tended to save that kind of thing, as it came in at Christmas time when she sent little presents home to her brothers and sisters. So she reached in and pulled it out, and as she caught the corner of the paper a small metal object fell from it into the depths of the box.

Ellen guessed what it was immediately. She reached for a stick and began poking away eagerly at the ancient residue of soot and dirt at the bottom of the box. She was so excited that she kept losing it again as she delved about. But at last she cleared the dirt away, and by leaning right forward could just reach it with her finger tips. When she had straightened up she shook it and rubbed away the dirt. She held it up to the light. It was a beautiful little amethyst pendant set in a circle of tiny pearls, with a second smaller amethyst hanging from it on a gold chain. Ellen could feel her heart pounding.

4. *AFTERNOON*

Ellen tore up the back stairs and forgot to listen when she got to the second floor. She narrowly missed bumping into Miss Frances who was just going into her room. Ellen stopped herself in time from calling out 'I've found it!', and went on up to her room to change into her afternoon clothes.

Rose was there fastening the bib of her apron with its broad white ties, looking at herself in the simple wooden-framed mirror that stood on the chest of drawers. Ellen told her, panting and breathless, about the discovery, and asked her if it would be all right to go to the mistress straight away to return it.

'I'll go and see, and if you wait for me at the top of the back stairs, I'll come out and tell you. But I should calm down, my girl. She won't be that easy to convince.' Ellen stopped, puzzled by Rose's words, but Rose had tidied her hair by this time and left.

So Ellen slipped off her brown apron, her white one and her collar and dress. It was a relief to take off her hot clothes. She would liked to have lain down on her bed for a few minutes, too, to rest her legs which were aching from the morning's work, but there was no time for that. She hung the brown apron up behind the door, put the dress back on its hook behind the curtain, and took down her black wool afternoon dress. She quickly washed in the drop of cold water left from the morning and put on her dress. Over it she put a fresh white apron, like Rose's only plainer, and tied this at the back of her waist in the same way as the one she had just taken off. Usually she enjoyed putting on her afternoon uniform, as it made her feel fresh and smart after the hard work of the morning. But she didn't think about that today. Her hair was so untidy after the morning's exertions that she had to start it all over again, unwinding the bun and picking out all the pins. At last Ellen had got her bun all back in place again, reasonably neatly, and tied her white afternoon cap on over it. This was small and pleated, with a lacy border and two long ribbons hanging down behind.

She took up the pendant and the scrap of tissue paper and ran quickly down to her arranged meeting place with Rose. She only had a few minutes to wait.

'You can see her now,' said Rose. 'In the boudoir. And mind you don't go passing the blame.'

Ellen still didn't understand Rose. Nervously straightening her apron, she went out on to the main landing and down the front stairs to the boudoir door. She tapped on it and went in. She knew this room, of course, from doing the fires, but she had never seen it in use before. It was obvious why it had become the main sitting-room for the family. It was smaller and more friendly than the drawing-room. But it, too, was full of knick-knacks and interesting objects, with soft, decorated hangings on the mantelpiece and on every piece of furniture, and displays of everlasting flowers under glass domes. There was a strange clock also under a glass dome, with all the works showing and just a little enamelled face.

'So you have something to say to me, Ellen.' The mistress was sitting in a little velvet covered chair by the fireplace.

'Yes mum, please. I found this,' she held out the pendant in the tissue paper, 'in the dust box when I was cleaning away after luncheon, please, and I thought. . . .'

'I see. I'll take that, thank you. I am very glad that you have thought better of your actions yesterday, Ellen. Repentance is a virtue, even if it can only be under pressure.'

'But I'd not seen it before this. . . .'

'It is much better that we should regard the matter as closed. And I think you had better not waste any more time. Poor Simmons seems to have been very busy today, getting ready for our little dinner this evening.'

Ellen stood outside the door for a second, feeling crushed. She went down the front stairs to the ground floor and slowly down the kitchen stairs. Her job and her future were safe, but she couldn't feel happy or even relieved about it. The mistress still thought she had taken the pendant.

Cook was very busy. She had no time to think about Ellen's story, and when she had heard it just said, 'Well, that's all over. Now take the other end of *that*, if you please.' *That* was an enormous pan, very shallow but about eighteen inches long and half as wide, partly filled with water. Cook was trying to lift it on to the top of the range. It was a *bain-marie*, and it was used in the kitchen on occasions when a large number of sauces were wanted for one meal. Cook would make the sauces in small saucepans during the course of the afternoon, and then stand the little pans in the *bain-marie* to keep warm until they were wanted. The water in the *bain-marie* kept the sauces at just the right temperature so they didn't get cold and form a skin, but they didn't go on cooking and therefore spoil.

'Now either get out of my way and do what you have to for that Rose, or set to and do something useful here. There's work for ten servants in this house today.'

Ellen went back up to the dining-room to find Rose. It had been arranged that she would spend an hour this afternoon with Rose, helping to set the

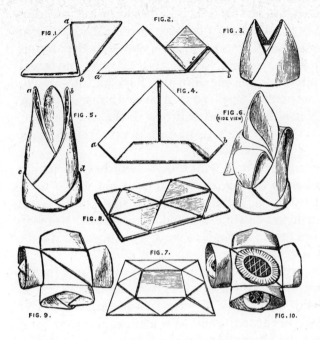

10   Method of folding table napkins from *Warne's Model Cookery*, 1879

table and learning what she had to do to wait on the guests. She didn't feel like being alone with Rose at the moment, but she knew she must.

Rose had already put the cloth on the table, and smoothed it over to perfection. Now she was laying out the silver from the plate basket which she held over one arm. Ellen waited for her to finish, to receive her instructions.

'I'd better show you how to fold a napkin, I suppose. Here, take one off the pile, and watch what I do.' Rose went through it slowly, but Ellen found it hard to follow, and had to be shown all the way through twice. The finished article looked more like a penguin than any water lily she had ever seen, but she didn't say anything. Eventually they produced six lilies that satisfied Rose, though she herself was responsible for four of them, and they set them in front of the places. There was a pile of plates from the best china service on the sideboard, and Rose gave her some to put round.

After the middle of the century the way of serving dinner had changed. The old-fashioned way was to put all the food on the table at once, savoury and sweet; then those empty dishes were replaced by a new lot, which made up the second course. That was fairly easy for the servants. The master and mistress would serve some of the dishes, with the servants passing the plates, and the guests would then help themselves to the rest, or indicate to the servant what they wanted. The new fashion, called *dîner à la russe*, was to serve each dish separately: this meant you changed plates and cutlery with each dish. Enough servants were required to serve each guest quickly while the food was still hot. Meals changed from two courses consisting of many dishes to eight or nine courses, each consisting of one main dish with accompanying extra dishes such as vegetables and sauces. That at least was the ideal arrangement: what most middle-class people like the Parkers did was to serve their meals in a mixture of the two ways, so that some things would be put on the table and served by the master and mistress in the old manner, and other things would be passed by the servants to each guest separately, in the new manner.

Rose told Ellen the different courses, and which one should go on which plate. By the time they had finished laying, each place setting had a total of three plates, with five more for each person on the sideboard. Ellen couldn't be present for all the courses, but she wanted to remember the way it went so she would know the next time she had to wait. She repeated it over in her mind to make sure she understood.

'Whatever you do, you mustn't speak unless someone says something to you first. And you aren't supposed to listen to the conversation: of course you *do* listen, because you've got to hear when they say they want something. But don't laugh at any jokes they tell, because it looks as if you're joining in, and you aren't meant to. Behave as if you're looking at them through a window, so you can see what they're doing, but not hear what they're saying. And believe me, you'd better see what they're doing, because if you let anyone wait too long before being passed what they want, the mistress will tell *me* off for it, and I'll let you know it afterwards. And be sure to scrub your hands before you come up with the first dish, because if your fingernails are dirty I'll send you right back down again.'

There were going to be six people altogether at dinner, the master and mistress, Miss Frances, a gentleman and his wife who were friends of the Parkers, and their nephew; after dinner they were all to go out together to a dance given by the parents of a friend of Miss Frances's.

It was the first proper dance that Miss Frances had been to, and Mrs Parker had had their dressmaker make her daughter a dress especially for it. Ellen had seen it hanging up in Miss Frances's room and she thought it was beautiful.

She didn't feel exactly envious of Miss Frances, more proud to have had some part in the great occasion. After all, she had been hard at work with Cook preparing the food they would eat, and she would be there to help serve it when the time came. Mr Parker's elder brother had been sending them lots of game recently, from the family estate in Yorkshire, and the dinner tonight was really based on these gifts. Ellen had been learning to pluck and draw various game birds, a job that she found disgusting at first, as very often the birds had been hung so long they were crawling with maggots. She had also been helping to make the jellies and custards that were now laid out in the larder.

Rose soon packed her off back to Cook. Rose's next job was to arrange the centrepiece of the table: she enjoyed that and wanted to do it her own way. She would make a little group of flowers round a silver ornament and trail pieces of an ivy-like plant called smilax between the plates; it gave her great satisfaction and she wanted to concentrate on it.

When Ellen got back to the kitchen there was a pleasant surprise waiting for her, the first of the day. It was a letter for her addressed in her mother's careful copperplate handwriting. Cook had propped it up on the mantelpiece above the range. Ellen decided to save it up to read tonight, when all the work of the day would be over.

Cook had planned the menu for tonight herself. It was written out and pinned up to the mantelpiece just in front of Ellen's letter. Ellen examined it carefully. She knew that planning menus was the most demanding part of a cook's job. You had to be really knowledgeable and experienced to do it well. She deciphered the foreign words, and tried to work out what the dishes were. Cook's menu looked like this:

Soupe Macaroni
Boiled cod and oyster sauce

Entrées   *Entrées*
Salmi of wild goose   Escalloped oysters

Saddle of mutton Portugaise

Potatoes   Broccoli

———————————————
Grouse

Cheese canapés   Isinglass jelly
Custard with cream   Volunteer's pudding

Apricot tart

The saddle of mutton and the grouse were already prepared and waiting to go into the oven at the right time. Cook had made the goose dish yesterday, to be heated up when the time came. The custard, the jelly and the tart were in the larder. So Cook still had to prepare the soup and the fish, the oysters, the cheese canapés and the puddings. The stock for the soup was waiting in an enormous pan on the stove, and the lemon sauce to go with the puddings was sitting in the *bain-marie* beside it. Cook was beating the pudding mixture when Ellen returned to the kitchen from the dining-room. She looked worried.

'The boy from the fishmonger hasn't come,' she said to Ellen, 'and I've got to have my four dozen oysters when I've finished this pudding. The sauce is waiting for them, and I'll have to get the scalloped oysters ready before I start the soup. Clear away those pans and bowls, and then you'd better go and see what's happened to him.'

This was unusual. Ellen scarcely ever had a chance to leave the house, and apart from her ordeal on the front steps every morning, hardly even looked into the street. She certainly didn't know where the fishmonger's shop was. But it was a real treat to be able to go out. She had never got used to being kept indoors all the time, after her country childhood when she had all the fresh air she wanted.

In the meantime, though, there was still a pile of washing up waiting for her on the end of the kitchen table, and she knew she'd have to get that done before she left. So she carried everything through to the scullery and set to work. More soapy water, more scouring, and now the added problem that her drying-up cloths hadn't had time to dry out since luncheon, and she seemed to be making things wetter when she used them instead of drier. But she got the pans and bowls put away, trying not to notice that since she had started that lot of washing up Cook had created a new pile of dirty things at the end of the kitchen table.

'Get your jacket on, and fetch one of those rush game bags from the cupboard under the stairs,' said Cook. 'It's not far, and I don't think even you could get lost. You don't need to give him any money, just say it's for Mrs Parker's house and the boy was supposed to bring them this morning. Four dozen, don't forget. And don't you talk to anybody. If you do get lost, pick a respectable-looking lady to ask.' She told Ellen the way twice over, and saw her out of the kitchen door and up the area steps. Cook was rather worried about sending her out alone, but she was more worried about her oysters. It was too late now to prepare anything else.

Ellen took a deep breath of the warm, dusty air of London on a mild early autumn day, and looked round at the street. Behind each front door, she realised, is a whole household, probably just like ours, with a tweeny and a cook and a Rose. She realised that she was so caught up in the daily round of *their* house that she never thought about the fact that there were hundreds of other households all around her, all with their dinner parties and their missing jewellery and worries exactly like hers. She never got a chance to talk to the other servants in the street, so she couldn't exchange stories with them.

At the end of their quiet street she turned the corner to the right, just as Cook had told her, and after a few yards found herself among a small group of shops.

The racket in the street here was dreadful, for it was a through road and there was all the traffic going in and out of central London as well as the carriages, delivery drays and carts of the people who lived and worked locally. The metal wheels and horses' hooves clattered and crashed on the road, and there was a tremendous shouting every time vehicles knocked into each other, which was frequently, or if someone was in someone else's way.

Ellen had to cross the road, and she was so bewildered by all the sights and noise, after her own quiet residential street, that she stood for some time just staring across, wondering how she could ever do it.

'Go down to the corner, dearie, and try it there,' shouted an old lady going by on the pavement with a battered handcart full of vegetables.

Ellen looked the way she was pointing, and saw that there was a crossroads a few yards farther on and pedestrians were crossing, braving the traffic in small groups. She went past the open door of a public house, recoiling at the hot beery smell which wafted out and avoiding some men who were having a heated discussion on the pavement outside; she took a quick sidelong look at the dresses displayed in the window of a ladies' outfitters next door, but didn't dare stop. The next shop, which was on the corner, was a pawnshop, and Ellen hurried past this too, without even wanting to look. She knew only too well what unhappiness was associated with a visit to one of these shops. Her mother had once had to take some clothes into Hadleigh, to get money on them at the pawnshop there: it was during one very bad winter when the farmer couldn't afford to hire the usual number of men, and Ellen's father hadn't been able to find any other work for nearly a month. Ellen remembered the awful hunger, and how ashamed her mother had been at the idea of pawning clothes, and how difficult it had been to make the money later to redeem them.

There were one or two people just stepping out into a gap in the carts and carriages, and Ellen joined them. She found herself on the other side of the street just outside the fishmonger's. There was no one inside the shop, so she plucked up courage and went in. The bell, on a curling spring attached to the door, went on ringing for several moments after she had got inside.

Behind the counter stood the fishmonger. He was small and neat, with a pointed nose, and was dressed in a dark blue and white striped overall with a white apron over it. He wore a flat straw hat.

Ellen picked her way across the sawdust-strewn floor to the counter and gave him Cook's message. She had to say it all over twice, because she spoke so quietly.

'One of my lads is off work today, and the rascal who was supposed to do his round for him must have forgot. I'll have a look out the back. I know I made up the order.' In a few minutes he came back into the shop with the neat brown paper parcel, now very damp, and Ellen held open her rush bag to receive it. It was heavy, like a parcel of stones.

'Please tell your cook I'm sorry for the mistake, and we won't let her down again. I'll send the account as usual, end of the month.'

Ellen left the shop, relieved that it had been so easy. What she didn't realise was that the traders who dealt with the larger houses in the neighbourhood did everything they could to keep their customers, and wouldn't have been unpleasant to Ellen in case Cook took her business elsewhere.

Cooks had a lot of power over the shopkeepers, because the large households they worked for used up a lot of food, and that meant they were important customers. Some shopkeepers even paid money to cooks, as a bribe to use their shop rather than their rivals'. When this happened the shopkeeper would add a little to the bill, to cover the cost of the bribe, and the mistress of the house, who paid the bills, usually didn't notice. Ellen's cook didn't do this; as a result she found she got even better service at the local shops. They were anxious to please because they didn't want to lose her.

Ellen now had to get the oysters home as fast as possible. She crossed the road quickly and made her way back through the crowds.

She reached their house, ran down the area steps, and tapped on the kitchen window. The glass was all steamed up but she could see Cook inside, turned to the range, stirring a saucepan. The pile of dirty dishes on the end of the table had doubled in size since Ellen left. Cook turned round and saw her, then disappeared through the kitchen door.

'Did he have them?' she asked sharply as she opened the area door.

Ellen told Cook what had happened, while she put away her jacket and opened the parcel on the kitchen table. Cook told her to get a bowl of water to put them in, and then handed her an oyster knife.

'Have you ever done this?' she asked Ellen, who shook her head. The oyster knife had a short stubby blade and a short, stubby wooden handle. Cook showed her how to hold it firmly, the butt of the knife against the heel of her hand, and force open the oyster with a quick twist.

'You be careful, you could take a couple of fingers off with that knife. Now, I want half of them opened straight away, for the sauce. You do that, and I'll get the puddings steaming. That Rose'll be down any minute for her tea tray, and I've not started it yet. All they ever do up there is eat. Disgusting I call it.'

Since three o'clock Rose had been answering the door. From three until six every day Mrs Parker would pay or receive calls. If Mrs Parker went out herself to pay a call Rose had to answer the door and tell the visitor that Mrs Parker was 'not at home'; in that case, the visitor would then give Rose a visiting card with her name and address printed on it.

Rose had to hold out a silver tray, called a salver, for the card. She wasn't supposed to touch the cards with her fingers. On the other hand, she had to make sure that the cards of the most important callers were left lying on the top of the pile. Sometimes Mrs Parker would be at home but wouldn't feel like seeing anyone. Then she would tell Rose at luncheon that she 'wasn't at home to visitors' that day, and Rose would have to tell any callers that her mistress was 'not at home'.

Once when Rose wasn't well, Ellen had to open the door to the visitors. It had been one of those days when all the routines break down, and everything had been muddled. Ellen didn't know that she should find out Mrs Parker's plans first, and when the callers, an old friend of Mrs Parker's with her two daughters, arrived, she left them standing on the doorstep while she went to find out if Mrs Parker wanted to see them or not. Mrs Parker was in the nursery checking Henry's clothes with Nurse, and couldn't see them, and by the time Ellen got back downstairs to tell the visitors that her mistress was 'not at home', they had been standing for a good five minutes in the rain. They hadn't called again for some time, and Ellen got into trouble from Rose about it the next day when Rose heard the story. Ellen dreaded the next time Rose was ill: luckily it didn't happen often. It was much worse if Mrs Parker *was* 'at home' because then you had to take the visitors up the front stairs to the boudoir, or the drawing-room, wherever Mrs Parker was sitting, and *announce* them. Rose knew the names of most of the Parkers' friends, as she had been with the family for nearly ten years, but Ellen would have had to ask

11   Tea in the garden

them their names, then throw open the door and say very loudly 'Mr and Mrs Jones'. And Rose had a good clear voice: Ellen thought her own soft little voice and Suffolk accent sounded awful. There were all sorts of things to get wrong: how should she announce the vicar? and if a lady called with her married daughter there were two names to find out, and then get the wrong way round.

It was much better in the kitchen. Sometimes if the guests came in their own carriage, or had a maid come with them, the coachman or the maid would come downstairs to the kitchen for a glass of beer while they were waiting. Cook enjoyed talking to these other servants, and Ellen would find an excuse to sit sewing, listening to the chat.

The upstairs callers only ever stayed about a quarter of an hour, and Rose would hover on the back stairs on the drawing-room floor. She had squeezed an old chair on the tiny landing of the back stairs there so she could sit down. When Mrs Parker rang the bell, Rose had to appear in the drawing-room to show the visitors to the front door, and if she had gone down to the kitchen each time she would have been exhausted by the end of a busy afternoon. But at about a quarter past four she went down to the kitchen anyway, to see to the tea tray. Cook had to get it ready for her. Rose would check the number of cups and plates, allowing one more than the number of visitors in case anyone else arrived, then carry it up to the drawing-room.

By the time Rose came into the kitchen to get the tea tray Ellen had opened twenty-four oysters and only cut herself twice.

She had made a tremendous wet mess on the kitchen table, though, and fragments of oyster shell were everywhere. Luckily Cook told her to spread out newspaper, so that it would clear up quite easily. But Ellen wasn't a very elegant sight, and Rose looked at the blood, the dark grey shells and the water with some disdain.

'I suppose we'll just have to hope for the best this evening,' she said haughtily, and looked round for Cook. Cook had gone off to the larder, which she often did about this time to avoid meeting Rose. She had left the tea tray on the side, with silver tea pot and hot water jug, milk jug and sugar basin with tongs. There was a plate of paper thin bread and butter on the tray. Rose adjusted the numbers of cups and saucers, and with great dignity picked up the enormous tray and made for the door. Ellen found herself wishing just for a moment that she would trip and drop the whole thing; but as soon as she had thought it she was sorry, because of the fuss that would arise from it. No one could wish that even on to Rose. As she thought about it, folding up the great bundle of soaking newspaper, she realised that Cook had been right when she said that Rose hadn't exactly helped her. After all, it had probably been Rose's fault in the first place, for throwing the pendant away by mistake. Rose had only got to say that. The mistress wasn't likely to be too upset at Rose making a mistake, so it couldn't really hurt her, and it would really make a difference for Ellen.

Mistake. *Was* it a mistake? Could Rose have done it on purpose to get Ellen dismissed? Ellen was horrified at the thought. Why ever would she want to do that?

When Cook came back a few minutes later, Ellen had scrubbed the kitchen table to its original spotless state, and washed her hands clean of all the mess. No one would have guessed what effort had produced the neat dish of shelled oysters standing in the middle of the table. Cook was almost impressed.

'That's not bad for a first try,' she said. 'If there's time, you can do the rest later on. That's harder, you have to have one good shell for each oyster, seeing as they're served in the shells. These ones just go straight in the pot.' And she tipped the hard won prize of Ellen's afternoon into the saucepan.

5. DRESSING FOR DINNER

Rose struck the big gong that hung at the bottom of the stairs in the main hall. It had a leather-covered striker, and the sound carried, gentle and insistent, through the whole house. Ellen's heart beat faster. It was the dressing gong, and it meant that the evening was now under way: in the next few hours would come the climax of all their work.

Ellen was back in the kitchen with Cook. Earlier, they had taken twenty minutes off for their own tea, and Ellen had eaten some bread and butter and cold chicken to take her through to supper, which they wouldn't have until after

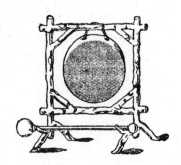

it was all over. Cook had just sipped at a cup of tea. She never ate when she was in full swing on a meal. She said that all the food put her off it herself. and Ellen could understand. Afterwards Ellen had taken a tray up to the nursery, for Nurse and the children, loaded with bread and butter, jam and cake. This was the children's last meal of the day.

Next Ellen had to start again carrying up hot water cans. She took the two for the nursery first, and then went downstairs again to get one each for the mistress and Miss Frances. Rose put the ladies' clothes ready on their beds: she would help the mistress to dress and Ellen would help Miss Frances. Ellen saw to fires in the ladies' bedrooms, and in the master's dressing-room. Then she had to fetch the nursery tray. She had just got back to the kitchen with the tray when the dressing gong had gone.

So Ellen made her way back to the top of the house, pausing at the 'public' landings as usual. She had to go to her own bedroom to get ready herself first. She changed the apron, and tidied her hair and cap, but she couldn't change anything else, as her afternoon dress was the best one she had. Ellen went down to the second floor. She knocked on Miss Frances's door and heard her call out, 'Come in!'

Miss Frances looked very nervous. She was standing by the fire in her cotton shift, fastening on her corsets. She seemed relieved when Ellen appeared.

'Ellen, please do up the laces for me. I'm sure I won't be ready in time.'

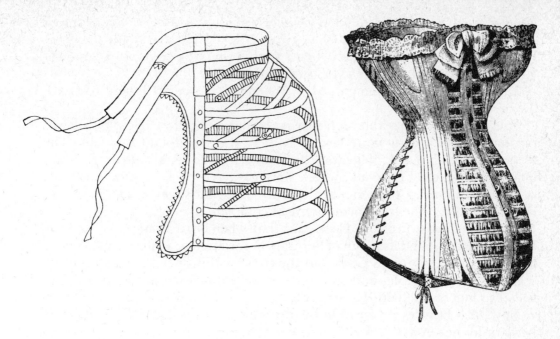

12a   The 'Canfield' bustle, 1888   12b   Corset from *The Milliner and Dressmaker*, 1879

Ellen took hold of the two laces at the back of the hour-glass shaped corset, and pulled, nearly jerking Miss Frances off her feet.

'Wait, I'll hold on to the mantelpiece,' said Miss Frances, and when she had got firm hold, Ellen tried again. She pulled until Miss Frances said that she couldn't breathe, and then tied them tightly. Over the corset they tied the boned frame which acted as a foundation for the dress. Bustles had come back in the last year or two and were now at the height of fashion. Over the framework they slipped another petticoat. Finally Ellen gently picked up the beautiful pale blue and white silk evening dress that had been lying on the bed, and Miss Frances put it on over all the foundations.

It wouldn't do up. They had to take off all the layers again, back to the corset.

'Try pulling harder, Ellen. It must be possible. Some of my friends get much smaller waists than that. I'll hold my breath!'

'Yes, Miss Frances. But it would never do if you fainted tonight.' But she did pull again, and they got it down by nearly an inch.

'I think that will be enough, Miss.' As Ellen looked up, she noticed that Miss Frances's face was rather pale.

'Would you like to sit down a moment, Miss?' Miss Frances moved stiffly to an upright chair by the bed. There was an armchair in the room, by the fire, but Ellen could see that Miss Frances wouldn't be able to bend enough for that.

'It didn't seem nearly so bad when I tried it on last week. Can I have got larger, do you think, Ellen?' Miss Frances asked.

'I daresay it's the excitement, Miss. When you're ready I'll help you with the dress again.'

This time they were able to fasten it. It had a very low neck, but it was modestly filled in with white lace, and there was lace too at the cuffs. The underskirt of white silk, delicately patterned in pale blue, was draped and looped with folds of blue silk, which were gathered back into the bustle. It made Miss Frances stoop forward slightly, but that was considered a very elegant posture. The transformation was complete.

Ellen liked Miss Frances. Cook said that when Miss Frances was a little girl she used to spend as much of her time in the kitchen as she could, getting in the way and talking to Cook and the tweeny. But since she had got older it hadn't been possible, and anyway she would have been embarrassed to spend so much time with the servants.

Now Miss Frances sat down at the dressing-table, so that Ellen could tidy her hair for her. A hairdresser had come in that morning to put it up and curl it, so all that was needed was for the odd wisps to be put back in place, and the little curly fringe at the front to be made neat again.

While she was sitting in front of the mirror, Miss Frances picked something up off the table. Ellen's heart sank when she saw it was the little piece of tissue paper that she had found that afternoon. Miss Frances unwrapped the pendant, and looked at it for a few moments before slipping it on a black velvet ribbon and tying it around her neck.

'Ellen, I don't think you ever meant to keep it. But what *did* you think you would do?'

'Oh Miss, I never saw it before this afternoon when I looked in the dust box. It just must have been thrown away by mistake. Really, *you* must believe me. The missus didn't give me a chance to explain. If only you'd tell her.'

'I will, Ellen, the next time I get a chance.' Pause. 'How awful for you.'

'Yes Miss, you see, it's because of my character. . . .'

'Yes, of course.'

Ellen could see it was no good going on about her problems. How could Miss Frances understand how important a character was? Ellen could only hope that she would remember to mention it to her mother sometime.

'Will that be all, Miss Frances?' Ellen was thinking of Cook and the steam-filled kitchen.

'Just tell me if I look all right, Ellen.' Miss Frances stood up and arranged her skirts around her. She held her head forward, her elbows slightly away from her body, and to complete the picture, had taken up her white evening

13 An afternoon dress in cream satin, about 1878

gloves and fan which Rose had laid out on the bed.

'Oh, Miss. Just lovely.' The folds of the dress hung perfectly and the little amethyst was just the right ornament. Ellen felt a pang of envy at the crisp bustle and layers of silk skirts, and she just stared for a moment.

'Thank you, Ellen. You can go now.'

On her way down, she stopped at the drawing-room floor to do the fires. They had almost gone out and Ellen had to spend some time reviving them.

Down in the kitchen Cook was moving fast. The soup was boiling, and she dropped in a scoopful of little pieces of macaroni, stirred the oyster sauce in the *bain-marie*, looked to see if the water in the large fish kettle had started to simmer, then turned round to the table to finish preparing the grouse for the oven.

'Get this apron on and take the oysters out to the scullery to open them. There's no room for all that mess here.'

Ellen went to the scullery, where the gas was already alight, and to her dismay saw that there was not much room there either. The draining-boards were piled with more dirty pans and bowls; Cook had been dumping them out there as she finished with them. There was no time to do anything about that now, so she cleared a space, spread out some paper, and got to work on the second lot of oysters. She was so practised at it by now that she got through them in no time, and went back to the kitchen proudly bearing a plate of twenty-four shells each containing one slippery little morsel.

Cook glanced at them. 'Put them down over there and then put the tureen to warm. The dish for the fish and the sauce boat are already warming. Then put the potatoes on to boil.'

Rose came down to the kitchen, but just as she appeared the door bell sounded. She had to go back up to open the door to the guests, take their wraps, and lead them up to the drawing-room to announce them. While they were waiting for Rose to come back, Cook and Ellen got the dishes together for the first course. Everything was ready for the performance to begin.

6. DINNER

As soon as Rose returned she, Cook and Ellen took up the covered silver dishes and set off for the dining-room. Rose led the procession up the kitchen stairs, across the hall and in through the dining-room. She had already lighted the gas in the ornate metal fixture hanging above the table, and the room was ablaze with its light. Rose showed them where she wanted the various dishes. The soup went in front of the mistress's place and the fish in front of the master's. The sauce boat for the fish was placed on the corner of the table next to the master. While Rose was arranging the table, Ellen mended the fire. Then Ellen and Cook withdrew to the kitchen again, and Rose went up to the drawing-room to announce that 'dinner was served'.

In the kitchen Cook was back at work on the entrées. Ellen stood nervously waiting for Rose to ring the bell, which she would do as soon as everyone was seated. She watched the row of bells on little springs high up on the kitchen wall, labelled 'Front door', 'Drawing-room', 'Dining-room', and so on.

'Ting-ting-ting.' Ellen was half way to the door before the bell had finished ringing and Cook called after her to be careful. She turned the handle of the dining-room door as quietly as possible, and tiptoed into the room. She crept round the edge, to take up her position at the far end. She didn't dare raise her eyes to look at the table.

'Tell me, Captain Osborne, how is your dear mother?' the mistress was asking in a loud voice. Ellen looked up cautiously. She could see the young man sitting on Mrs Parker's left, his uncle opposite him.

Next to Captain Osborne was his aunt, Mrs Eliot, and opposite her was Miss Frances. She could see the top of the master's head over the silver centrepiece. On the sideboard behind him there was a display of the family silver that wouldn't be used in the meal; candlesticks, salvers and teapots, arranged by Rose as part of the decoration of the room.

Rose stepped forward to take the lid off the soup tureen and pass the ladle to the mistress. She put the lid on the side, took a soup plate, gave a nod to Ellen and went back to the table, waiting at the mistress's left. Ellen also took a plate and stood behind Rose. The mistress served a plateful and Rose moved silently round the table with it to Mrs Eliot's place, where she offered it to her with her left hand. Now it was Ellen's turn. She held out the plate. Mrs Parker ladled in some of Cook's soup and Ellen carefully carried the

14 A dinner table, from *Mrs Beeton's Household Management*, 1888

plate round to Miss Frances's chair. Miss Frances leant to her right and Ellen gently put down the plate from Miss Frances's left, holding her breath in her efforts not to slop the contents up the side of the plate. It was all right, and she stood back in relief. She felt like skipping back to the sideboard for the next plate.

In the meantime, Rose had carried a plate round to Mr Eliot. All the while there had been a brisk conversation in progress. The master and Mrs Eliot were listening to Miss Frances, and Mr Eliot was telling the mistress something about his nephew's parents' house down in Wiltshire. Ellen couldn't make out all they said. She wasn't used to the way they spoke, and she couldn't let her attention wander from her duties long enough to concentrate on the conversation. She took the next plate round to the master, and then she went to stand behind the mistress. Rose took away the tureen when Mrs Parker had served herself, and put it on the sideboard with its lid on top. Then she went to stand behind the master.

Ellen looked at the group of diners. Mrs Parker and Mrs Eliot were dressed more soberly than Miss Frances, Mrs Parker in dark blue and Mrs Eliot in brown. Ellen could only see the bodices of their dresses, which were elaborate concoctions of satin and lace, both with high necks.

The men were in black evening suits with tail coats; the tails were hanging down through the backs of the chairs. Their shirt fronts were glistening like snow, and Ellen noticed how they had to hunch themselves forward to take in spoonfuls without risking the tiniest splash. They were all dressed more smartly, she knew, than they normally would be at a small dinner, because they were going on somewhere else afterwards. Ellen was impressed by the way they knew how and when to take up and unfold the waterlilies that she and Rose had made for them. Also by the way they all unhesitatingly picked up the right spoon to start on their soup.

Rose caught Ellen's eye, and Ellen noticed that the diners had put down their spoons by their empty plates. They cleared away the soup plates, and then served the fish in the same way as the soup, except that this time it was Mr Parker who filled the plates from the silver dish in front of him.

While the diners were starting on the fish, Rose went round with a bottle of wine and filled a glass by each place, and Ellen made a neat pile of the dirty plates, putting the dirty spoons on a special tray. She then picked up the plates and tiptoed to the door, her heart pounding for fear of dropping them. Somehow she managed to open the door, go through and close it again without disaster. She did nearly stumble at the bottom of the kitchen stairs, but by then she felt on home ground. She put the plates on the draining-board in the scullery, and went through to the kitchen. Cook was poised over the oven.

'How's it going, then?' she asked.

'Oh, it's not so bad as I thought,' replied Ellen.

'*So* far,' said Cook, giving her a look. 'Now clear the kitchen table off and get the entrée dishes ready.' Ellen did as Cook asked, and they both stood looking up at the bell marked 'Dining-room'. In a few moments it went. Then Cook and Ellen started to take up the next course. They had to make two journeys, with the enormous covered dish containing the saddle of mutton, the two entrées in their silver dishes, the vegetables and the china plates themselves warm from the oven and wrapped in a cloth. Rose carefully arranged the mutton and the vegetables on the table, leaving the covers on. Cook took the dirty fish plates downstairs. Ellen went to the sideboard and waited until Rose was ready.

This was the difficult bit. The guests had to choose between oysters or goose. Rose went first, offering the oysters to each of the guests in turn. If they accepted, that was all right, but if they refused Ellen had to be ready with the goose dish and hold it for them while they helped themselves, making sure that the serving spoon and fork were in the dish so that they could easily be picked up. Ellen was 'backing up' Rose as a footman would back up a butler in a grander house. All the time the next course was waiting on the table, under its silver covers.

This was the first time Ellen was on her own, having to think for herself.

All went well until they reached Mr Eliot. He chose goose, but as he turned to help himself, he knocked the dish and some of the sauce spilt on his coat-sleeve. Rose fetched a cloth from the sideboard and it was soon cleared up, but as she passed Ellen she whispered fiercely, 'You'll be sorry for this tonight.' Ellen couldn't have whispered anything in her own defence, because they might notice at the table. She was really frightened by the incident and felt her knees trembling. But they managed to finish serving out the entrées without any more mishaps.

Ellen stood, still shaking slightly, behind Mrs Parker's chair. As she recovered she started to take in what was being said at the table.

'My husband enjoys a day's shooting: in fact, he'll be off next week to spend a few days with his brother, who owns some very fine grouse moors,' Mrs Parker was saying to Captain Osborne. Mr Parker joined in from the other end of the table.

'Yes. Go down every year. Fine lot of sportsmen in those parts. You a shooting man, Captain?' And they began to discuss the pleasures of a day with a gun. When this was finished Mrs Parker leant forward to address Mrs Eliot.

'The difference this year is that I'm sending Frances as well, to enjoy herself with her cousins. I shall be quite lonely on my own, with only the children. You must come and see me as often as possible . . .' and again the conversation moved on.

Ellen gradually absorbed this piece of information. It was the first she had heard of this visit. What difference would that make for them? Just at that moment Rose caught her eye again, and they had to start taking away the dishes.

The master carved the mutton. Rose and Ellen took round the plates, and then saw that everyone was served with vegetables. Ellen took the dirty dishes from the last course down to the kitchen, where she found Cook turning out the puddings from their individual tins on to a serving plate. Ellen asked her about what she had heard.

'Yes, he does that every year. I expect you'll be sent with them this time, as someone will have to look after Miss Frances. Wish they'd send that Rose and give us all a rest.'

Ellen heard this in amazement. Just then the bell rang and they couldn't talk any more. Cook took the dish of grouse out of the oven where it was waiting for this moment. She surrounded it with game chips (potato crisps) which she had made the day before. Ellen carried it upstairs, and gave a little tap at the dining-room door with one free knuckle. After a moment Rose let her in, and took the dish from her. Rose had cleared the table of the last course, and there was another pile of dirty plates on the sideboard. Rose put the grouse on the table, in front of the master, and then both she and Ellen fetched

STOCK-POT.   BAIN-MARIE.   STEW-PAN.

BRAIZING PAN.   BLOCK TIN SAUCEPAN.   BOILING-POT.

DOUBLE, OR MILK, SAUCEPAN.   IRON SAUCEPAN, WITH STEAMER.

OMELETTE PAN.

SAUTÉ-PAN.   FRICANDEAU PAN.   PRESERVING PAN AND SPOON.

SALMON KETTLE.   TURBOT KETTLE.   FISH KETTLE.

15 Pots and pans, from *Mrs Beeton's Household Management*, 1888

16 *Mistress*. 'Oh, Gwendolen, whatever *have* you done!'
Gwendolen. 'It's all right, m'm. I 'aven't 'urt myself!'

plates and again took them in turn round to the guests. By now Ellen was used to the atmosphere of the room. As soon as she could, she slipped out with the dirty plates and carried them downstairs. There she found Cook assembling the last course. On the kitchen table she had put a large tray, and on it laid dishes containing a jelly, a baked custard and an apricot tart. There was a space for the plate of puddings and their sauce, which were keeping warm. Beside the tray were arranged pieces of toast with slices of cheese laid on top of them. Cook had stoked up the range and opened the flues so that the fire was burning fiercely, in order to heat the oven to its hottest. When the bell went next, she would put the cheese canapés in the oven just long enough to melt the cheese, then carry them up to the dining-room while Ellen went on ahead with the tray.

When they were both back in the kitchen, Ellen went out to the scullery to take stock of the washing up. The sink was full of the pots and pans that Cook had dumped there. The draining-board was covered with dirty plates. The floor around the sink was piled with dishes and plates. She put her present load down on the floor, went out and shut the door on the whole thing. She would probably be there until midnight washing them up, but now she had other things to think about.

Cook was getting ready a tray of cups and saucers. While she started on the coffee, Ellen went up the back stairs to check the drawing-room fire. It had nearly burnt itself out, but she put on some more coal and shifted the pieces cleverly until it started to crackle and flames came. Then Ellen swept the hearth, using the little brush with a silver handle that hung next to the fireplace, and put everything in order. She looked round to see that the rest of the room was tidy. Rose was busy providing finger bowls, filled with scented water for the diners to rinse their fingers in, and wouldn't get a chance to come back here before the ladies came upstairs, so Ellen was responsible for seeing that everything was ready. She only had to straighten a few cushions, and clear a table to take the coffee tray.

Cook had made the coffee and was pouring it into a silver coffee jug when Ellen got back to the kitchen. She was only just in time as the bell went again almost straight away. That was Rose signalling to Ellen that the ladies had left the table. Ellen was to give them a few moments to get settled in the drawing-room, and was then to take up the coffee tray. Meanwhile Rose would see to the men, clearing the table, removing the tablecloth and putting on it the decanters with port and burgundy from which they would help themselves, as well as dishes of dried fruit and nuts.

So Ellen waited three minutes by the kitchen clock. Then she picked up the tray with its cups and jugs, remembering for a second how she'd wished earlier that Rose would drop hers. What a crash it would be, she thought now, and the idea made her more nervous. Very carefully and slowly she went up the back stairs, both flights as far as the drawing-room floor. Carefully she pushed open the green baize door and started to cross the landing. Mrs Parker had left the drawing-room door open and the ladies were sitting at the back of the room, so they couldn't see Ellen coming. Ellen could hear their voices as she crossed the hall, and couldn't help hearing what they were saying.

'Well of course I'd decided to send the tweeny with them,' Mrs Parker was telling Mrs Eliot. 'But then there was all that fuss this morning, and I'm not sure now it's such a good idea. Dear William has got that lovely collection of silver—how could I ever forgive myself if I were responsible for sending a dishonest servant into the house?'

'Mama,' Ellen could hear Miss Frances say, 'you know that it wasn't certain she had taken it.'

'Well I know that's what *she* says, but Simmons tells me that she's never been too sure about her since she came, and I *always* think that Simmons knows about these things. Anyway, she was very clumsy at dinner.'

'You can't be too careful,' Mrs Eliot observed. 'I had a housemaid once who . . . oh, my dears, *pas devant!*' She had caught sight of Ellen coming round the door with the tray. Ellen put it down carefully on the table that she had cleared a few minutes before. She felt everyone in the room was holding their breath until she left. She didn't wait for Mrs Parker's permission, but turned and fled from the room.

7. ROSE'S STORY

'I don't want to go with them,' Ellen managed to say at last to Cook. 'But why should Rose take my character away? I've never done her any harm.' Ellen had burst into tears when she got back to the kitchen and was sitting at the kitchen table, her head in her arms.

Cook didn't stop her work to comfort Ellen, but she did speak to her gently as she put things away.

'That Rose is an odd one and there's a few things I could say to her. Don't carry on. Maybe Rose wants to go with Miss Frances herself. The last tweeny that we had went to help out at that house, and the missus there took a fancy to her and asked her to stay on. There wasn't anything our missus could do about it, see. It would have been rude to complain, as the master's only the younger brother. If Rose went and got taken on there, that would be promotion for her, and she'd get more money out of it.'

'But I'd rather she went,' said Ellen. 'I don't want to be on the house side.'

'But you've never told *her* that have you? And you might change your mind if you got the chance to be a housemaid. You're a tall lass; they like them tall. You'll notice the ones on the house side usually are taller than the kitchen side.'

Ellen stood up and was tying on the large brown apron to start the washing up when Rose came into the kitchen.

'There you are,' she said crossly to Ellen. 'What did you mean by making all that mess at dinner. I've never seen such a clumsy girl. It makes twice as much work for me. I don't know what they teach scullery maids these days but you don't seem to know the first thing about your job.'

'Leave the girl alone,' Cook interrupted. 'You aren't so perfect. If you don't lay off I'll tell her why!'

Ellen looked at them in amazement.

'I've nothing to be ashamed of.' Rose's voice was beginning to get shrill. 'I've worked for my own, I was done wrong, and I'm not the first, nor won't be the last if it comes to that.' She turned on her heel and left the room. The company were getting ready to go out, and Rose had to fetch coats for guests and family.

Ellen and Cook were left standing in the kitchen. Cook worked off her feelings on Ellen. 'Don't just stand there. You've got enough to do, haven't you?' she said crossly, and then turned fiercely to carry on clearing up her things.

Ellen put all the pots and pans that were in the sink on to the floor, and put some hot water from the copper into the sink. She took a deep breath, and started on some plates. Cook put her head round the door.

'Don't forget all that dirty silver up in the dining-room still,' she said. Ellen sighed and dried her hands on her apron.

She crept upstairs, listening at the door from the back stairs. The guests were still standing talking in the drawing-room, so she slipped across the hall and shut herself in the dining-room.

When the women had left them to go to the drawing-room, the men had sat with their port and smoked cigars. The room was still full of the exotic smell of the smoke. Ellen took up the tray of dirty cutlery from the sideboard, listened at the door, then scampered down the hall to the back staircase. The company were just beginning to come downstairs, so she had taken a risk.

There was an enormous amount of washing up to do, and she started again with resignation. Rose came in after a while, to fill a basin with hot water. She had to wash the glasses used at dinner, which were too fine to be entrusted to a tweeny. She took the bowl back into the kitchen, without saying anything to Ellen. When she returned later to empty the bowl she still didn't speak.

Ellen was tired by now. When Cook called her in to supper she had not nearly finished, and she gladly took off her damp brown apron. In the kitchen Nurse and Rose were already sitting down at the table. Nurse usually ate in the nursery, but was downstairs this evening because they had been too busy to do her tray. Cook was carving the mutton left over from the dining-room. She had warmed up the leftover vegetables and put them on the table; tonight they would have more than their usual bread and cheese. Ellen sat down next to Nurse, and this time she did pour herself some beer from the mug on the table; she hoped it might revive her a little. There was a sense of anticlimax in the group; the performance was over and there was nothing left but a lot of weary clearing up to be done.

Rose was still angry, and didn't speak at all during the meal. She finished as quickly as she could, and left them. She had to go and turn the beds down and put out the night clothes. Later Rose would have to sit up for the Parkers, to let them in and take their coats whatever time they chose to come back. Then she would have to help Mrs Parker get ready for bed.

When Rose had left, Nurse asked Ellen what was going on. Ellen looked to Cook.

'I told her that if she didn't lay off the young one I'd tell about the little boy.'

'What little boy?' asked Ellen.

'You'd better tell her now, hadn't you?' Nurse laughed. 'There's no secret left.'

'I didn't know she was married, even,' said Ellen.

'She's not,' said Cook. 'That's the trouble. And I suppose the child's not

17   Jennie and baby, and Esther: photograph of two housemaids by A. J. Munby, 1881

so little now either. He's looked after by a lady in Ealing, and Rose goes there on her half-day. His father was a footman at her last place, somewhere up in Yorkshire. He couldn't marry Rose and he wouldn't have anything more to do with her when he heard about the baby. Well, she has to work to support the child, and she never would have got a place if she had the boy with her. Service was all she knew, and it gave her a roof over her head and just enough money to provide one for the baby, if only she could get a good place. There's lots do the same. But you've got to keep it a secret, see, because they won't employ anyone who's immoral. I found out about it when the lady who's looking after him came here once when he was ill and she needed more money (or so she said) to buy him medicine. If you ask me that kind make fortunes out of people like Rose.'

Ellen was shocked and even more upset now. Not shocked that Rose should have a baby: she knew that happened to girls in service quite often. But shocked to think that all these years Rose should have been able to suffer so much and keep it to herself.

She went back to the washing up in different mood from the one in which she had left it. She couldn't forgive Rose for all the unkind things that she said and did, and the idea that Rose might have let her, Ellen, lose her place and her character quite unjustly made her blood run cold. But it was different, somehow, seeing it against a background of all Rose's worries, about her job, her little child, and the sadness of only being able to see him for an afternoon every two weeks. Rose had to devote her life to the whims of those upstairs. She didn't even have any friends that Ellen knew of.

The last pan finally done, she splashed cold water round the sink, to wash away the sand, and dried the few things left on the draining-board. She went through to the kitchen, turning out the gas before she went. She looked up to the mantelpiece and noticed that the clock said 11.15. Cook had taken down her menu, but there was the letter, propped against a little ornamental jug that had belonged to the last tweeny and had been left behind. Cook had gone upstairs. Ellen was just about to open the letter when the kitchen door opened. It was Rose.

'I've turned down the beds, but the fires will want doing, and the water cans will have to be changed. After that you'd better go to bed. There won't be any time off tomorrow, I can tell you that now.'

Ellen paused for a moment before leaving. She would have liked to say something friendly to Rose about what she had learnt. But when she looked at her she realised that she would never be able to get through the tough shell that Rose had acquired. So she put the letter away in her apron pocket and went upstairs to start on the fires.

All she had to do at this time of night was to make sure that the fires in the dining-room, the boudoir and the drawing-room would safely burn themselves out, and that the fires in the bedrooms would stay in until the mistress and Miss Frances were in bed. Rose would take another look at them later on. The gas was still alight in the hall, and although Rose had extinguished all the other lights in the house, that one gave Ellen enough to see her way by. She collected the hot water cans from the bedrooms of the mistress and Miss Frances, and took them down to the basement again. There she consulted Rose.

'Even if they're by the fire, the water'll be cold by the time they get in.'

'All right,' Rose said, 'I'll take them up later on. That's what you want I suppose.'

'No, it's just. . . .'

'Go on, up you go.'

Ellen took her candle from the scullery, lit it using a paper spill which she lit in turn from the fire in the range, and left Rose sitting by the kitchen table. Rose had brought some mending down with her, but she was too tired to do it and was just staring in front of her.

Ellen went up the back stairs, and then quietly up the stairs through the upper floors. There was a glimmer of light from under Nurse's door : she must be sewing by candle-light. There was no light from Cook's room and Ellen could hear the heavy breathing of someone who has fallen into a deep sleep after a hard day.

It was cool and fresh in the attic after the hot kitchen, and Ellen found that a relief now, though in winter it would turn very cold. She put the candle on the chair by her bed, and spread out the letter on her knees, sitting on the bed itself. The clock struck 11.30.

Her mother had written news of the family. William had passed the test for the sixth standard and would be leaving school at the end of the month. She wanted him to start an apprenticeship at the blacksmith but Father hadn't the money to pay for the indentures so they would probably take him on up at the farm. Margaret was being a good girl, and helping with the little ones, and Mrs Jennings said she'd take her as a general servant, as she had Ellen, when she left school next year. The others were all right now, though they had worried about Arthur catching scarlet fever from the family down the hill.

'Last week Father was in Hadleigh for the market and he met a young fellow who asked after you. He said he worked up at Bewick Hall and knew you there. Father said he was a footman. We all laughed to think our Ellen Annie had a follower.'

Albert! Ellen smiled to herself, pleased to hear of her friend. That was nearly the end, just a few more scraps of news about people in the village, and about the house. Next Sunday afternoon, her afternoon off, Ellen would stay in her room and write her answer.

Now she got undressed. She hung up her dress carefully, and folded all her other clothes neatly, putting them over the back of her chair. She got into bed and blew out the candle, stretching out between the cold sheets. She could feel her muscles loosening all over, and waited to drop off, as she always did, straight away. But tonight it didn't happen immediately.

She imagined Miss Frances at the dance, surrounded by young men all dressed like Captain Osborne. She thought how grown up and confident Miss Frances seemed compared to herself. But she had done things Miss Frances hadn't done: she earned her own living, and had left home at thirteen. When Miss Frances went away next week, it would be the first time she had been separated from her family, and she was seventeen now.

It had been a very unusual day. Generally life ran to the same plan day in, day out, over the year. The unusual days stood out like landmarks. The next one wouldn't be until the older boys came home from school at Christmas time. That would make more work. Not only were they untidy, but they liked to tease her. After Christmas, there was nothing but the spring cleaning to look forward to. That was a real upheaval; the family would probably go away for a couple of weeks, and the servants would have to turn the house upside down, doing out all the rooms. They would be on 'board wages'. Mrs Parker would pay Cook twelve shillings a week for each servant to cover wages and food. Cook knew how to lay out the money so that there might be a bit left over for each one of them and she had already promised Ellen to make some of her favourite home dishes, like pigs' trotters and pease pudding, which were never made for the gentry. During spring cleaning the downstairs rooms were to be redecorated. The joiner and painters would be in for several weeks. Ellen wondered what it would be like with strange men coming in and out of the kitchen and no fear of meeting 'them' in the front part of the house.

Then in April there would be Miss Frances's presentation. Cook said there would be lots of parties: hard work, but at least exciting. And then, perhaps, she could take her week's holiday. She was saving the fare to go home out of her wages. But that was a long way off. In the meantime, they kept to their routine.

What was tomorrow? Wednesday? That wasn't too bad a day. She and Rose would turn out the study. That was easy for it was hardly ever used. Friday was worst, when they had to do the flues. . . .

She did drop off, eventually, but not before she'd heard the clock strike twelve. A little later she was conscious of Rose coming to bed, but it didn't really wake her. She dreamt that her mother was in London, telling Mrs Parker that her Ellen Annie was a good girl really, though she had started to have followers. Then she stopped dreaming, even, and just slept.

Cook shook her shoulder roughly. 'It's quarter to six. Thought I'd better wake you,' she whispered. 'Hurry up and get dressed. I can't do all the work myself.'

71

18 Easton Lodge, near Dunmow, Essex. The staff, about 1890

8. THE NATIONAL SCENE

BACKGROUND

The most striking fact about domestic service in Victorian England is the number of people involved. Although only one in five households at the most employed servants, towards the end of the nineteenth century there were over a million women and girls in private service, which means that almost one in three girls between the ages of fifteen and twenty was classified as a domestic servant. Everywhere servants were taken for granted as one of the facts of Victorian life.

TABLE I   NUMBER OF INDOOR DOMESTIC SERVANTS AND OTHER
FEMALE OCCUPATIONS 1851–1911

Date	Indoor domestic servants[a]	Civil servants, nurses teachers, shop assistants[b]	Textiles: all branches and types[c] (to nearest thousand)
1851	751,541	89,139*	635,000
1861	962,786	194,438	676,000
1871	1,204,477	250,604	726,000
1881	1,230,406	316,001	745,000
1891	1,386,167	445,624	630,000
1901	1,285,072	561,985	610,000
1911	1,271,990	791,242	636,000 (1907)

[a] Census of Occupations, England and Wales.
[b] Lee Holcomb, *Victorian Ladies at Work* (David & Charles 1973).
[c] B. Mitchell and P. Dean, *Abstract of British Historical Statistics* (CUP 1971).
* Census of Occupations.

This huge population of servants was partly the result of changes in farming methods which released women and girls from work on the land.[1] In towns and cities more and more families employed house servants as the shop-keepers, manufacturers, professional people and those living off unearned income became wealthier and wanted a more elaborate style of living. Wealthy non-industrial towns like Brighton and Exeter and the West End of London had the highest proportion of servants. But where there was other work, for example, in Leicester where there were stocking factories, fewer women and girls went into service.

In the eighteenth century wealthy households employed almost as many

[1] Ivy Pinchbeck, *Women Workers and the Industrial Revolution, 1750–1850* (Frank Cass 1967).

A Day in the Life of a Victorian Domestic Servant

Four households from the 1851 census

1.

Household position	Age	Occupation
Sir George Henry Smythe—head	67	MP, baronet
Eve, Lady Smythe—wife	71	
Charlotte White—granddaughter	17	Scholar
William Player—servant	42	Butler (married)
Thomas Pitts—servant	50	Coachman (married)
Susan Pitts—servant	48	Cook (married)
Henry Pitts—servant	14	Stable boy
Mary Anne King—servant	37	Lady's maid
Sarah Glasse—servant	21	Lady's maid
Susan Pudsey—servant	27	Housemaid
Rebecca Abbey—servant	21	Housemaid
Susan Bushbrook—servant	19	Kitchen maid

2.

Household position	Age	Occupation
William Howard—head	50	Solicitor
Elizabeth Howard—wife	35	
Alfred Howard—son	3	
Catherine Howard—daughter	2	
Mary Howard—daughter	1	
Elizabeth Howard—daughter	1 month	
Sarah Jumper—servant	32	Cook (unmarried)
Betsey Leech—servant	24	Housemaid (unmarried)
Emma Radford—servant	16	Housemaid (unmarried)
Mary Herbert—servant	67	Monthly nurse

3.

Household position	Age	Occupation
William Leech—head	42	Chemist and druggist
Jane Leech—wife	33	
William Leech—son	7	
Ellen Leech—daughter	1	
Frederick Hole—apprentice	14	
Ann Claydon—servant	23	Housemaid
Rose Gower—servant	16	Nursemaid

4.

Household position	Age	Occupation
James Bland—head	24	Railway guard
Harriet Bland—wife	22	
Walter Bland—son	3	
James Bland—son	3 months	
Emma Williams—servant	12	Nursemaid

men as women for work indoors. During the nineteenth century the proportion of men slowly declined as new jobs were created in factories, offices and schools. Men were then only employed as footmen and butlers, by very rich families. By the 1880s parlourmaids were being substituted for men. There was a growing feeling that indoor men servants were a luxury not many people could afford. The cost in wages and food was high and they also created problems in the household by flirting with the women servants and refusing to be strictly disciplined. The men preferred to work outdoors in the stables and gardens: they were not under such close personal supervision and they could live in their own homes.

By the 1850s middle-class families, often in imitation of the upper-class round of Court, Balls and the London Season, began to expect more complicated meals and household routines. Instead of having one main meal at about 3 or 4 p.m. and a light supper in the evening, people dined at 7 or 8 p.m. Afternoon calls, musical evenings to which guests were invited, dinner parties, or 'At Home' days meant that the mistress of the house had to be free from housework and looking after the children. The Victorians saw these customs as an important part of their duty to their family and community.[2] The size of the house and the quantity of furniture, crockery, cutlery, curtains, carpets and knick-knacks considered appropriate to one's station increased steadily. Thus there was a demand for more servants and in the wealthier households people wanted more specialised servants like cooks.

TABLE 2   THE EMPLOYMENT OF SPECIALISED SERVANTS
IN ENGLAND AND WALES 1851–1871[a]

	1851	1871	Increase %
Females			
General servants	575,162	780,040	35.6
Housekeepers	46,648	140,836	201.9
Cooks	44,009	93,067	115.5
Housemaids	49,885	110,505	121.5
Nursemaids	35,937	75,491	110.1
Laundry maids	n.a.	4,538	n.a.
Total	751,641	1,204,477	56.6
Males			
Indoor general servants	74,323	68,369	−8.0
Grooms	15,257	21,202	+39.0
Coachmen	7,030	16,174	+130.1
Total	96,610	105,745	+9.5
Total			
(male and female)	848,251	1,310,222	+54.5

[a] John Burnett, *Useful Toil* (Allen Lane 1974), p. 138.

[2] L. Davidoff, *The Best Circles: Society, Etiquette and the Season* (Croom-Helm 1967).

As standards of cleanliness and comfort rose, even the families of skilled working men often had a young living-in servant to do the scrubbing and dirty work as well as baby-minding. Victorian respectability was based very much on being able to keep clean. Mothers liked to dress their daughters in clean white pinafores and their sons in clean white shirts. Clean doorsteps and front paths, shiny brass door knockers and sparkling windows with fresh white curtains were especially important to impress passers-by, neighbours and friends. It was very difficult, particularly for a woman with a large family, to manage all this without the help of a servant.

Why did girls go into service in such great numbers? One of the main reasons was the lack of opportunity for other work. With the decline in agriculture and work that was done at home, such as spinning, women and girls were limited to a few overcrowded occupations: textile manufacture, dressmaking and millinery. There was a growing feeling that women ought not to be working in mines, fields or factories, and at the same time working men were afraid that women might compete with them for such jobs. It was felt that ideally girls should stay at home until they married and had husbands to support them. T. J. Barnardo wrote in 1889:

'The East End of London is a hive of factory life and *factory* means that which is inimical to *home* . . . they [the factory girls] are early thrown upon the world to "fight for their own hand", there is bred in them a spirit of precocious independence, which weakens family ties and is highly unfavourable to the growth of domestic virtues.'[3]

As the daughters of working men and women had to earn their living, it was thought that the best job for them was to be living and working in respectable middle-class homes. In this way domestic service came to be seen as the ideal occupation for girls and single women. Many parents were glad to have their girls in respectable service, although some of the mothers who had been in hard places themselves were often determined to help their daughters find other jobs.

RECRUITMENT

In the early nineteenth century children went into service at what seems to us a very early age indeed—usually when they were about ten years old, although some were even younger. But we must remember that it had always been the custom for many children to go to live in other people's houses from

[3] T. J. Barnardo, '*Something Attempted, Something Done*' (published by the offices of the Barnardo Institution, 1889), p. 30.

quite an early age as apprentices or servants and, in any case, children did start work when they were very young.

TABLE 3   AGE OF PRIVATE DOMESTIC FEMALE INDOOR SERVANTS: ENGLAND AND WALES[a]

Date	Under 20	%	Over 20	%
1851	265,883	38	441,749	62
1861	372,399	42	512,565	58
1871	476,554	40	727,923	60
1881	528,367	43	702,039	57
1891	556,779	40	829,382	60
1900	449,271	38	743,608	62
1911	399,875	32	372,115	68
1921	137,156	24	425,571	76

[a] Census of Occupations.

Children heard about their first place through local shops or post offices or parents, friends or older sisters already in service. The schoolmaster or vicar might be asked to recommend a school-leaver for a vacancy. Many of these 'petty' places as general helpers in the homes of shopkeepers, schoolmasters, railway officials, etc., were near enough for the children to live at home and go to work from 7 a.m. to 6 p.m., usually six days a week. At about the time Ellen was in service most children would have been to school from the age of three to about thirteen (although many left as soon as they could gain a 'leaving certificate'). They learnt to read and write, do some sums and needlework. It was important for servants to be able to read and write. A report written in 1870 says of Eliza Lewis, a girl from the workhouse, that although she 'never gives a pert [cheeky] answer, at age 14 [she] cannot read or count change or tell the time so she will have to leave her place'.[4]

By about the age of fifteen many of the boys who had done odd jobs such as knife and boot cleaning, left for non-service jobs. The girls at that age might go on to a sleeping-in place farther away from home. Servants' places were sometimes advertised in newspapers or registry offices for servants. These offices were run for profit and were not licensed or controlled in any way until the twentieth century. Both the servant and the employer had to pay a fee to the office and there was no guarantee that either the job or the servant was at all suitable. Some registry offices were fronts for recruiting prostitutes. Experienced servants tended to rely on information about jobs from other servants or tradesmen.

The employer could ask for a reference or 'character' from the previous employer. Servants had to rely on gossip from other servants or accept the

[4] From the report of the Visitor for the Metropolitan School District, 1870, Greater London Record Office, SMSD/179.

conditions of the situation as they found it. Legally a 'character' was a *privileged communication*—the employer was not required to tell the servant what was in it or even to give a character at all. Many employers tried to be fair in giving references because they realised that the servant's livelihood was at stake, but there was always the temptation to give a good reference to a bad servant to get rid of her, or, on the other hand, to refuse a reference out of spite. Servants, too, might be tempted to forge written references when they were 'short', that is, without a reference.

It was the custom for both employer and servant to give a month's notice to end their agreement. If the employer wanted the servant to leave immediately a month's wages had to be paid. If the servant left without notice, she forfeited her wages, so 'working out the month' after notice had been given by either side could be very unpleasant.

CONDITIONS OF SERVICE

The amount of lifting and carrying that servants did, especially in houses with basement kitchens and several floors, required strength as well as energy. A full copper hod of coal weighs between 28 and 30 lb.; an average bath jug of water about 30 lb. (Try counting the number of journeys Ellen made during the day from the basement kitchen. Notice that she was almost always carrying something up at least one flight of stairs.) Before the late 1850s prams were unknown and although small hand carts were sometimes used for older children, the nurse, nursery maid or general servant girl had to carry the young child in her arms during the long afternoon walk, producing 'the twisted form and unequal shoulders of young nursemaids'.[5] (The average eighteen-month-old middle-class child of the 1880s weighed 26 lb.)

Like all people who work in the home, servants were particularly prone to accidents such as falls on stairs, burns and scalds. Many employers were not interested in home safety as they were not personally at risk or responsible for the servant, at least until servants' injuries were included in the Workman's Compensation Act of 1907. Anaemia and digestive and nervous complaints seem to have been the most frequent illnesses among servants, caused by lack of fresh air, monotony and very long hours of work.

Because households that employed servants were run for the comfort of the family and the display of the house to visitors, there was little interest in 'labour saving' as we know it. There was a great deal of variation in the plumbing, heating, lighting and cooking facilities that created the conditions of the servants' work. These varied not only according to income and standard of living but also because of the middle- and upper-class habit of

[5] J. T. Arlidge, *The Hygiene, Diseases and Mortality of Occupations* (London 1892), p. 16.

renting houses and moving frequently. 'Modernisation' of plumbing, for example, was considered too expensive for the tenant, while the landlord, who did not live in the house himself, was not particularly interested either.

In the earlier part of the nineteenth century servants had no regular time off but had to ask permission to leave for even short periods of time. Time off

19   'Time off.' Photograph by A. J. Munby, about 1880

was given as a reward for work done or, with younger servants, withheld as a punishment. By the time Ellen was at work servants were given a half-day off on Sundays, starting after lunch. Ellen was expected to go to church on her Sunday afternoon off, although this was not enforced as rigidly as it had been a generation before. She also had one day off a month starting after breakfast. Her work had to be done before she could go, and if the family was late, she would have to wait to finish cleaning and washing up. Places with more than one servant were better as they could 'cover' for each other. By about 1900 one other evening a week had been added. Ellen would also have one week's holiday a year when she could go home to see her family if she could save the fare; later on this was increased to two weeks.

Residential servants received their food as well as lodging, and usually had a money allowance instead of the beer, tea and sugar given earlier in the century. Out of their wages they had to find clothes and boots as well as fares and postage. Uniforms were not regularly worn by female servants until about the 1850s. Even after that date, in modest households where there was only one servant, she would usually wear her own dress plus the cap and apron that wives and daughters also wore in the house. By the 1880s servants in a house like the Parkers' would be expected to have a cotton 'print' dress, very often blue or lilac coloured, for the morning and a black light wool dress for the afternoon. These would be worn with special caps and aprons showing the rank of the wearer: housemaid, cook, parlourmaid, nurse. Men servants had their uniforms or *livery* provided by their employer. These were often in the style of the eighteenth century with knee breeches, silk stockings, ruffled shirts and, in the largest houses, powdered wigs. Butlers, however, wore tail coats and housekeepers usually wore black silk dresses; they were the most important servants and therefore did not have to wear uniforms.

With the expense of providing these clothes, it was difficult for girls like Ellen to manage on five shillings a week.[6] Servants often wanted to send money to help out at home, and when they were getting married they would try to save towards their own home. But if they were ill or between situations they had to support themselves from their savings, and unless they could go home they had to pay rent. Some servants would work for nothing to keep themselves in board and lodging between jobs. A few lucky ones might stay in hostels specially provided by charities such as 'The Female Servants' Home Society for the Encouragement of Faithful Female Servants' (established 1836).

Some of the groups organised among working people, such as the Friendly

---

[6] Twelve old pence equals one shilling: twenty shillings equal one pound. A loaf of bread cost five to six old pence. A pound of sugar cost two old pence, a pound of beef about five old pence. A pair of women's shoes—indoor shoes, not boots—cost about six shillings.

Societies, encouraged servants to save money; a few were founded particularly for them such as the Servants' Provident and Benevolent Society. If a servant managed to develop some skill, for example as a cook, she might earn considerably higher wages than a young girl or an older general servant. But, as in so many occupations, the really top positions were taken by men, for instance as chefs, who were often French or Italian.

TABLE 4   THE WAGES OF FEMALE DOMESTIC SERVANTS
IN LONDON IN 1895

Age	Servants in upper- and middle-class families[a]		Girls from workhouse[b]	
13	—		£5	16s
14	—		£5	18s
15	£7	2s	£6	16s
16	£8	14s	£7	16s
17	£9	18s	£9	0s
18	£12	2s	£10	4s
19	£13	10s	£11	0s
20	£15	0s	£11	10s
21–25	£17	8s	£12	4s
26–30	£19	18s	£12	18s
31–35	£21	12s	£17	14s
36–40	£21	18s	—	
40+	£24	12s	—	

[a] Charles Booth, *Life and Labour of the People of London*, 'Industry' vol 4, 1903.
[b] Metropolitan Association for Befriending Young Servants, *Report*, 1894.

Note The wages of servants were higher (a) in houses employing more than one servant (b) the older the servant (c) the more specialised the servant, i.e. cook, lady's maid, housekeeper (d) in London as compared with the rest of the country. Thus while Ellen started as a single servant to a shopkeeper in Suffolk at £2 10s a year, Cook at the Parkers' would be earning about £20 a year. (Clara Collet, 'Report on the Money Wages of Indoor Domestic Servants', *P.P.XCII* c. 9346, 1899.)

It is interesting to note that Mrs Parker paid twelve shillings a week board wages for each servant while the family was away from home. This meant that Ellen's keep was calculated as being twice her cash wage. In a household like the Parkers' the food was good and plentiful. At a time when the price of food was relatively low, as it was in the last quarter of the century, this seems usually to have been the case. It was in households with very tight budgets, such as those of artisans, tradesmen, schoolmasters, etc., or in lodging houses, that servants went short of food.

Although some employers at all levels were very strict about rationing out food to their staff and would even lock up the larder and keep the keys themselves, many employers preferred to think of servants as part of the household. Their keep was considered as part of the household expenses and their cash wages as only a small part of the reward for their work.[7] This feeling was reflected in the very slow change from paying wages every quarter to paying them every month, when in other occupations wages were being paid weekly and were often calculated hourly or by the piece. Some employers let their servants work without wages for weeks, either because they forgot to pay them or because they were short of ready money.

Sometimes employers raised their servants' wages after a certain number of years but this was in no way guaranteed.[8] It is difficult to compare servants' wages with those of other occupations because of the value of board and lodging; and many girls working in factories and workshops also lived at home and had their expenses partly paid by their parents.

The cost of travel meant that many servants might not see their families and friends for months or even years, although many would walk for long distances to do so. For example, in the 1890s a housemaid at Long Melford, Suffolk, used to walk to Bury St Edmunds and back on her day off—a distance of twelve miles—to see her mother and take her some of her soap ration. (Ex-servant interviewed by author.) Young servants were often very homesick as well as lonely.

Servants slept in the kitchen or in cupboards under the stairs in the early 1800s. Later on they were given the attics as bedrooms although men often continued to sleep downstairs to act as guards against burglars. After 1900 there were moves to improve the cold, damp condition of servants' rooms in an attempt to attract more girls into service. But employers often continued to forbid their servants to display pictures or personal belongings in their bedrooms and considered it their right to look through servants' belongings. Servants were often forbidden to sing or laugh at work or play about in any way. They were expected to do their work noiselessly and remain invisible unless actually doing a job, to stand in the presence of their employer, never to speak unless spoken to, and to walk out of the room backwards. If they broke or damaged anything in the house they were made to pay, the sum being deducted from their wages. Even though this was illegal it continued in practice. Employers were not legally obliged to care for a servant who became ill, although most employers kept their servants on through short illnesses. Longer periods of illness were much more serious as the servant often had nowhere to go to get better.

Of course servants did meet other servants and have good times. One

---

[7] Domestic servants were specifically excluded from the Truck Acts of 1831 through 1887 which made it an offence to pay workers with goods instead of cash.

[8] The worst off were those who like Rose had someone else to support. It was estimated that it cost a minimum of five shillings a week to board a child out in 1871. Report from the *Select Committee on Protection of Infant Life*, 1871, vol. VII.

20   Maid talking to the carrier at Grinkle Park, Yorkshire, 1885

woman remembers that when their employers were away on holiday 'we would roll up the carpets, Liza would play the piano and we would have a regular beano'. (Interview.) On their days off servants would go to tea gardens, for walks, to visit friends and relatives or, in the cities, to music halls. But the need to be back on duty at 9 or 10 p.m. often cut short their leisure activities and there was an increasing shame about admitting to their friends that they were 'only a skivvy'. In many situations, too, employers tried to enforce a 'no followers' (male friends) rule, which meant that girls had to meet their boyfriends secretly.

Because servants lived in their employers' home their whole lives came under the eye of their master and mistress. Some employers simply left the servants to get on with their work, especially if there was a housekeeper, a butler or other 'upper' servants to keep order and see that the jobs were done. But many employers, especially in the earlier part of the century, felt it was their duty to supervise the way servants dressed (black bonnets for church), the way they spent their money, who their friends were or where they went on their days off. They had very strict rules to keep their servants in order, gave them religious books to read and made them join in family prayers.

As many young servants came to the cities, especially London, from country districts, and had few friends, the employers' care and concern were important. But employers also felt that they had a right to control the girls' lives, at least within the house. They also usually expected a great deal of hard work, and relations between masters, mistresses and servants were often marked by bad feeling on both sides. It was not until the 1860s that it became illegal to strike a servant, and beating, slapping and teasing servants went on well into the later part of the century.

There were very few attempts to organise servants into trade unions. They were too scattered in private houses, their relations with their employers were too close and personal and they moved around too much for this to be possible. Some employers were worried by the fact that servants had nowhere to go on their days off if they were too far from home. They were especially afraid that young girls would be tempted into affairs with young men.

To supervise the girls' behaviour and to give them somewhere to go on their afternoons off, upper-class ladies founded several organisations. In the 1870s the Metropolitan Association for Befriending Young Servants or MABYS was started in London to help workhouse girls sent out to service. Lady visitors called to check that the mistresses were satisfied with the girls and that the girls were being treated reasonably. (A clue to the girls' attitudes to these efforts may be found in their own name for the society, 'Mind And Behave Yourselves'!) At about the same time Mrs Townsend founded the Girls' Friendly Society which was to cater for all working girls not just orphans or workhouse girls. These organisations had rest homes for servants who were ill and hostels for those without a place, and ran non-profit-making registry offices. They provided entertainment like Bible and singing classes. They were staffed by volunteer ladies who stressed personal contact with the girls, fellowship through religion and reverence for the Royal Family. Unlike trade unions they were not run by the servants themselves. (In 1885 the Girls' Friendly Society had 100,141 members, a little over half being domestic servants.)

EFFECTS OF SERVICE

Contact with servants was one of the ways in which middle- and upper-class children were introduced to their social and economic world. They had to

" PLEASE 'M, DO YOU TAKE IN POOR LITTLE GIRLS ? "   AN INDUSTRIOUS LITTLE MAID

A GIRL BEFORE AND AFTER RECLAMATION

21 These pictures appeared in the magazine *The Graphic* on 16 January 1875

learn very early in life that servants were different from themselves. They
walked, talked, ate, even smelled differently and there was a great gulf
separating the two groups. Some children were very fond of the servants in
their home and found their way of life fascinating and a relief from the very
formal life of the middle-class family. It was an adventure to sneak down into
the kitchen, to beg tit-bits of forbidden tasty food from the cook, play cards
and games or just listen to the servants talking. But some parents did not like
contact between their children and the servants.

As Ellen noticed, many employers felt uneasy about their servants.
Employers were afraid that their personal problems or the economies they had
to make to maintain their style of living would be revealed. After all, servants
were in a position to blackmail their employers or even let thieves into the
house.

Although employers knew that sooner or later most girls would want to leave to get married, it was in their interest to keep them as servants for as long as possible. Yet when the girls left to marry many employers wished them well and might even give them a gift such as a set of hair brushes. If they left to take a better job or for a change, however, employers were usually annoyed or angry at what they felt was unexplained restlessness.

Because service was considered the only respectable occupation for girls, and because it gave them a home as well as a job, all girl orphans and all girls living in the workhouse for other reasons (their parents might be away, or too poor or too ill to keep them) were prepared for domestic service. Girls who were thought to be too wild, or dirty or inefficient were sent into laundry work; the others were often given extra training in the homes of the institutions' staff as unpaid servants before being sent out to a place. It was very difficult for workhouse or orphanage girls to find places in larger households. Many of them suffered from bad eyes, deafness, weakness and other effects of a hard childhood and found the work of a general servant very heavy. Yet many of them worked in such places or in lodging houses as 'slaveys'.

The expectation that somehow domestic servants were always 'girls', and not really adults, made the position of older single women who stayed on in service difficult. There were few groups to which they could belong, for if they moved with their employers or changed jobs they lost contact even with their local church, one of the few organisations readily available to them in their limited time off. And in old age or illness, as the Parkers' nurse feared, they often had nowhere to go. An inquiry by the Poor Law Commission found that three-quarters of all domestic servants who needed help from the state had to be taken into the workhouse:

'In the main these domestic servants are single women who have never possessed a home of their own and who, when no longer able to maintain themselves, are obliged to seek indoor relief.'[9]

The majority of domestic servants did marry, although relatively late by our standards. At the time Ellen was working, a typical servant would be about twenty-five when she married. She would have been in service about twelve years and would have had between three and five different situations. Service took girls away from the control of their parents and local communities. It gave them opportunities for travel, but loneliness was one of the prices paid for this freedom. As a result, they often became involved in sexual relationships which could never lead to marriage. The lonely monotonous

---

[9] *Royal Commission on the Poor Law*, 1910, Lo. 53, p. 89.

Girls going out to Service.

In the earnest hope of encouraging girls in the Village Home to aim at a higher standard of conduct, and at the same time to prevent those who do badly from sharing, as they have hitherto done, in those benefits which only the well-conducted deserve, the Director has laid down the following conditions upon which alone in future Village Home girls will be placed out in service.

All girls who have reached their thirteenth birthday are placed in one or other of four divisions, according to character and conduct. The conditions of their going out to service are determined by the class in which they stand. A special review of these classes is made every six months, and the names of girls are transferred from any one division to any other as they have shown improvement or the reverse.

These four classes are as under:—

FIRST DIVISION All girls who on attaining their sixteenth year have a record of conduct and character which has been uniformly good for two years, will be eligible for going out to service at once, or as soon as suitable situations can be obtained for them. They will be furnished with an oufit of the first class, value £5, which will become their own, free of any charge, if they keep their first situation twelve months. Furthermore in the event of their keeping their first situation twelve months with a good character, they will be entitled to receive a special prize.

SECOND DIVISION Girls who have frequently given way to ill temper, disobedience, insolence, laziness or other grave faults within two years of their going out to service, cannot be placed in the first division; but if a resolute endeavour is observed in them to overcome their faults, and if, during the last twelve months of their stay in the Village, there is decided improvement, they will be placed in the second division, and receive a second class outfit, value £3 10s., which will become their own property on the same conditions as in the first division. Second division girls will also receive a prize if they keep their first situation with a good character, for twelve months.

THIRD DIVISION Girls who up to the time of their leaving for service continue to exhibit bad conduct, ill-temper, self-will, disobedience or insolence can only be placed out in the third division, the Mistress being informed of their faults. They will receive a third class outfit, value £3, the whole of which must be paid for out of their own wages. A girl in the third division will not be eligible for a prize till she has been two years in service, and has earned a good character.

FOURTH DIVISION Girls who are found to be dishonest, habitually untruthful, violent and uncontrolled in temper, vicious, unclean in their personal habits, will not be sent out to service under ordinary circumstances, nor will they have an outfit, but will be dismissed from the Village in disgrace or sent to a School of discipline.

GIRLS' VILLAGE HOME, ILFORD.   *T. J. BARNARDO,*

22   Rules for girls going out to service, from a Barnardo Girls' Village Home in Ilford, Essex

life in service meant that girls were vulnerable to the attentions of the master, the son and visitors to the house, or other men who saw them in the street and offered them treats in return for sexual favours. Living in the same house as the men made it difficult for girls not to become sexually involved and they would be afraid that if they told the mistress what was going on they would lose their job.

Although, in public, middle-class Victorians were horrified if they discovered that their maid was even flirting with men in the house, in private it was admitted that many boys had their first experience of sex with the maids in their own families or the families of friends. Of course if the maid became pregnant she was discharged from her job. Sexual relations with fellow servants, or with boys met casually on a day out, could result in a very serious situation, and 'Rose's story' was by no means unusual. Maids had little opportunity to get to know much about the young men they met and a girl could not be sure that her boyfriend would marry her if she became pregnant. Often a girl might be afraid to risk losing the security of a situation in service and would try to find some way of leaving her baby with relatives or a baby minder. However, when the abandoned corpses of new-born babies were found, particularly in suburban areas, it was assumed that they had been left by servant girls.

It is not surprising that many girls would go out with men in return for a good time—for presents or a bit of money. Girls like this were known as 'dolly mops'. But servants also turned to full-time prostitution, either between situations or as a permanent means of earning a living. For it must be remembered that even good jobs in service could come to a sudden end if the family fortunes changed or the breadwinner of the household suddenly died. In such cases the servant lost both job and home at the same time.

Masters and mistresses claimed that domestic service taught working-class girls proper methods of housekeeping. Was this true? It is very difficult to know. Many of the skills servants learned were not much use in working-class households and few servants were responsible for keeping the accounts, which was vital for anyone running a home on a small wage. It is true, however, that girls in service did seem to learn how to organise their day, how to fit jobs in and do several at the same time, which is one of the most important aspects of running a home.

After they married girls who had been in service had few ways of earning money. They could not go back to living-in service because they were expected to look after their husband and children, so they took casual day labour as cleaners or chars or, if they were lucky, occasionally helped out their former employers when there was extra entertaining or spring cleaning. Many also either took in washing or went to wash in their employers' home, heavy work which was very badly paid. The only other way to make money was to take in lodgers or to do unskilled 'sweated' work at home like sewing shirts or making matchboxes. What Victorians refused to recognise was that almost all wives of working men had to work to earn money at some time in their lives. Either they had to support themselves and their families (when their husband was ill, out of work, away from home, had deserted the family or was dead) or at least to supplement very low, irregular earnings. (See 'The National Scene' in *A Day in the Life of a Victorian Factory Worker*.) A girlhood spent in domestic service was of little practical use in facing this basic fact of economic life.

POST-VICTORIAN CHANGE

The decline in the employment of living-in servants, which began at the end of the nineteenth century, was given a boost by the First World War when 400,000 women and girls left service for factory work. Many never went back. After the war the less wealthy households (those where the husband was a skilled workman, a clerk, teacher, shopkeeper—or even a doctor or a solicitor) employed fewer or no personal servants. The large households seem to have carried on much as before, although by the 1930s even the upper-classes had modified their very elaborate style of living. Families preferred to put their money into goods, such as cars, and the decline in family size meant fewer children to care for in smaller homes. As other occupations began to offer shorter hours and opportunities for recreation, servants became even more dissatisfied with the very long hours and strict discipline that were part of living in their employers' households. Employers began to feel that they had a responsibility for making their servants' lives less monotonous and more agreeable. In the years between the wars many employers were glad to get rid of the whole problem of having 'strangers under their roof'.

Many households began to employ a daily servant or charwoman paid by the hour. But as a result much of the work that servants had done fell on wives, especially as it was now considered respectable for daughters to earn their living when they left school instead of staying at home and helping in the house until they got married. The need for middle-class wives to spend more time and energy cooking, cleaning and looking after the children perhaps contributed to the continuing belief that the most suitable work for women was taking care of their homes and families. The wide acceptance of this belief in the late 1920s and 1930s was very disappointing to those who had fought so hard for independence and votes for women.

Since that time social life has become much more informal. Clothing, furniture and household decoration are all simpler. There have been many developments in household technology—instant hot water, modern heating systems, electric appliances such as the vacuum cleaner, the washing-

23a 'Enterprise' Irons. Sad-irons with interchangeable handle, 1871

23b 'Vowel Y' washing-machine and mangle, 1897

23c Insulated ice-box, 1900

23d The 'Wizard' vacuum cleaner, 1911. This was operated by two servants

machine and the refrigerator. But the way in which the household is organised has not changed. It is still women who run the home. And even though more and more women at all levels of society have paid jobs outside the home they still expect and are expected by others to carry the main burden of shopping, cooking, cleaning, washing and ironing clothes and caring for children, the sick and the elderly. Wives are expected to do this, for the most part, without help and without pay.[10]

[10] Ann Oakley, *Housewife* (Allen Lane 1974).

Further Reading

Best, Geoffrey, *Mid-Victorian Britain 1851–1875* (Weidenfeld and Nicolson 1971) (World University Paperback)

Burnett, John, *Useful Toil: Autobiographies of Working People From the 1820s to the 1920s* (Allen Lane 1974)

Davidoff, Leonore, *The Best Circles: Society, Etiquette and the Season* (Croom-Helm 1973)

Dawes, Frank, *Not in Front of the Servants* (Wayland 1973)

Horn, Pamela, *The Victorian Country Child* (Kineton: The Roundwood Press 1974)

Hudson, Derek, *Munby: Man of Two Worlds* (Thames & Hudson 1972)

Kitteringham, J., *Country Girls in Nineteenth-Century England* (Ruskin History Workshop, Pamphlet Number 1)

Powell, Margaret, *Below Stairs* (Pan Books 1970)

Steel, D. J. and Taylor, L., *Family History in Schools* (Phillimore Press 1973)

Thompson, Flora, *LarkRise to Candleford* (Penguin 1973)

Index

Accidents 78
Accommodation for servants 13, 82
Afternoon calls 50–2, 75
Agencies 30, 77; *see also* Recruitment
Apprenticeships 70
'At Home' days 75

Bains-maries 44
Barnardo, T. J. 76, 87
Bathrooms 25; *see also* Washing
    arrangements
Bedrooms
    cleaning 27; preparation 67; servants'
    13
Beer allowance 40
Between maids 13
Board and lodging 80; *see also* Wages
Board wages 71, 81
Boilers 19
Breakages 82
Breakfast
    family menu 26; nursery menu 25;
    servants' menu 26–7; *see also* Food
Bustles 55
Butlers 75

Carpet cleaning 34
Chamber pots 28
Class distinctions 84–5
Cleaning materials 19
Cleaning routines 27–8, 30–1; increased
    standards 76
Coffee 64
Conditions of service 78–80
Cooking range 16
Cooks 75; duties 16, 33; training 37
Corsets 13, 54–5
Court presentations 24, 71

Dinner
    changes in meal times 75; fashions of
    serving 45–6; menu 47; parties 75;
    serving 59–62
Domestic servants
    attitudes of employers 84–9; conditions
    of service 78–80; declining numbers
    89; dress 13, 80; jobs after marriage
    88–9; moral problems 69, 86, 88;
    numbers employed 11, 73; physical
    strength 78; problems of old age
    23–4; recruitment 76–8
Dress
    formal 54–7, 60–1; of domestic servants
    13, 80; paid for from wages 80;
    servants' afternoon uniform 43

Education 77
Employers
    attitudes to servants 84–9; supervision of
    staff 83–4; types 73
Employment
    of men 75–6; of women 76, 88–9; *see
    also* Agencies; Recruitment
Entertainments 83
Entrées 47, 61
Evening dress 54–7, 60–1

Family prayers 26
Fares 80, 82
Finger bowls 64
Fires 19, 25, 27, 40, 59, 64, 69
Food for servants 27, 81
Footmen 75
Friendly Societies 80–1

Game birds 46
Gas lighting 16
General servants 70, 77; duties 17